GOLF IN OREGON

GOLF IN OREGON

Historic Tales from the Fairway

BOB ROBINSON
FOREWORD BY PETER JACOBSEN

Charleston · London

THE
History
PRESS

Published by The History Press
Charleston, SC 29403
www.historypress.net

Copyright © 2012 by Bob Robinson
All rights reserved

First published 2012

Manufactured in the United States

ISBN 978.1.60949.648.7

Library of Congress CIP data applied for.

CONTENTS

CONTENTS

FOREWORD

My earliest memories of golf in Oregon are of accompanying my father, Erling, and brother David to Portland Golf Club for the Portland Open Invitational in the 1960s. I can remember watching Jack Nicklaus, Arnold Palmer, Billy Casper and Bob Rosburg—and for the first time in my life, I became aware of the PGA Tour and what it meant to be a professional golfer. Up to that point, all I knew about the game of golf was that my dad liked to play it.

Like my father, I quickly developed a love for the game, and soon I was caddying for him and his friends at Waverley Country Club in Southeast Portland. As a caddie, I not only learned how to play, but I also learned the rules and etiquette and developed important social skills, like how to get along with people of all different ages. Most importantly, I learned how to respect others.

When I was a senior at Lincoln High School, preparing for the upcoming state tournament at Glendoveer Golf Club, I remember reading the *Oregonian* and seeing that the golf writer Bob Robinson had predicted that Peter Jacobsen would win the high school tournament. I thought to myself, "Wow, I can't believe a guy like Bob Robinson even knows who I am." Funnily enough, I did win that tournament and then went on to play collegiate golf at the University of Oregon.

After I turned pro and experienced playing golf around the world, I began to realize how much I had been influenced by watching the pros play at events like the Portland Open and the 1969 Alcan Golfer of the Year Championship, which was held at Portland Golf Club. How exciting it was for me, as a kid, to watch them play shots that actually counted—for real money.

It was the realization and reflection of how much I had been influenced by golf in the state of Oregon that helped us create the Fred Meyer Challenge in 1986. We wanted to bring back the excitement that surrounds having in-person access to some of the greatest players in the world, and Bob was there to show his support along the way. Bob was always there, right at the forefront of Oregon golf. He was honest, fair and, above all else, supportive of Oregon's and the Northwest's favorite sons. Players like John Fought, Jeff Sanders, Kent Myers, Mary Budke, Casey Martin, Brian Henninger and Bob Gilder; Seattle's Mike Reid and Fred Couples; and local heroes like Mike Davis, Bunny Mason, Pat Fitzsimons, Craig Griswold and Ralph Dichter.

As for Oregon's golf courses—I'm a huge believer that the courses in Oregon are underrated! From traditional designs like Portland Golf Club, Waverley Country Club, Columbia Edgewater Country Club and Astoria Golf and Country Club to the more recent and modern additions like Bandon Dunes Golf Resort, Oregon Golf Club, Pumpkin Ridge, Running Y Ranch and Brasada Ranch, these courses and more are all fantastic places to play. While I'm fortunate enough to have played almost all of the courses that Oregon has to offer, my favorite course in the state remains the track at Waverley Country Club, where I grew up. Close seconds include Old Macdonald at Bandon Dunes, Tokatee Golf Club in Blue River and Brasada Canyons Golf Course at Brasada Ranch.

I would like to thank Bob Robinson for his support and contributions to the game of golf in Oregon throughout the years, as well as his commitment to supporting players of the game, young and old, amateur and pro. His dedication surely helped build and strengthen the love that we all have for this great game of golf.

—Peter Jacobsen

PREFACE

It's strange how chance happenings can have a major influence on a person's career. Such was the case for me a couple years after I joined the sports department staff of the *Oregonian* in the fall of 1961.

I was at my desk, doing research for a story, when I overheard another reporter talking to executive sports editor Don McLeod about a possible assignment change. The reporter had been covering golf but was interested in switching to an open beat covering the Portland Buckaroos hockey team. As the conversation continued, I heard only snippets of what was said, but I could tell that McLeod was going to grant the request.

Anyway, as soon as their meeting was finished, I casually walked over to McLeod's desk and said, "I understand that the golf beat is open. I would like to have a shot at it." He grinned, obviously aware that I had been listening in on his conversation with the other reporter. "Now how did you know about that?" he said.

He didn't wait for a reply, instead asking me a couple questions about my knowledge of golf and my interest in it. Apparently satisfied with my answers, he told me I could have the assignment.

Thus began a long run for me as a golf reporter and columnist. I had a couple interruptions when I had other assignments, but I had the golf beat for most of the next thirty-five years before my retirement in 1999. Even after that, I continued to write a weekly golf column, "Golf Talk," for the *Oregonian* for the next five years.

My coverage centered on golfers and tournaments in Oregon and the Pacific Northwest, but I also had the opportunity to cover the world's finest men's players in twenty-four major championships and two Ryder Cups. On the distaff side, I attended more than forty LPGA tournaments, including five majors.

I anticipated that I would enjoy covering golf because so much of it would involve a closer relationship between writer and participant than is the case in most sports. I particularly enjoyed it when I could delve into a subject's personality and background as part of a story. Covering golf offered me that chance even more than I expected.

As with any work assignment, there were times of frustration on the golf beat. But honestly, not that many. For the most part, I had a long run of enjoyment covering golf.

Over the years, I kept an extensive clipping file of some of my stories and columns. I used that file extensively in writing this book. I hope that the reader will enjoy reliving the excitement of some of these events and personalities as much as I have in writing about them.

ACKNOWLEDGMENTS

This project never would have gotten off the ground without the gracious assistance of many. I give thanks to them all, including photographers Michael Lloyd of the *Oregonian* and Tom Treick, Jon Ferry, Wood Sabold and Eric Yaillen of the Oregon Golf Association. I'm also grateful to the Pacific Northwest Golf Association, the Pacific Northwest PGA, Portland Golf Club, Astoria Golf and Country Club, Peter Jacobsen Sports and Jeff Sanders Promotions for their assistance.

Aubrie Koenig, my commissioning editor, was wonderful in keeping my attitude positive through some struggles with the publishing process. Lastly, I give special thanks to my wife, Donna, for her patience, and to my grandson, Jean-Paul Wallis, whose digital technology intellect carried me through formatting and delivery.

THE DUDE—ONE OF A KIND

B ob Duden deserved a better fate on that miserable, rainy day at Astoria Golf and Country Club. But there was no denying that he had signed an incorrect scorecard, and he was disqualified from the 1968 Oregon Open.

At the twelfth hole of the afternoon round of a thirty-six-hole final day, Duden had driven his ball behind a small tree. In his typical style, he quickly chipped out sideways and then played his third shot toward the green. He made a bogey. Unfortunately for him, amateur Pat Fitzsimons, keeping Duden's scorecard, didn't see the chip-out and wrote down a par. Duden didn't catch the error when he turned in his soggy card.

The error was costly because the seventeen-year-old Fitzsimons won the tournament by two shots, with Duden in line for a tie for low pro and a check for a little more than $500.

"I hated pointing out the mistake to him," said tournament official Dale Johnson at the time. "It was such an awful day, and he had played so hard. But he was a great sport about it. Never complained. Just nodded and walked away."

It was one of my early experiences in covering Duden, and I was impressed with the class that he showed in this time of frustration and embarrassment. Later, I would come to realize that that was what he was all about. The game was his life, but he never considered himself bigger than the game.

The record books of Pacific Northwest golf are clogged with Duden's name. He won a record twenty-three major titles—including eight Oregon Opens—before his death in 1995. He played the PGA Tour periodically

Bob Duden hits a drive in a 1962 tournament, the year he won one of his eight Oregon Open titles. *Courtesy of Pacific Northwest PGA.*

in the 1950s and 1960s, winning an unofficial event in Las Vegas and tying for second in three official tour events between 1959 and 1964.

Before that, while still an amateur, he won a historic forty-two-hole championship match against Ralph Dichter in the 1949 Oregon Coast Invitational at the Gearhart Golf Links.

Then there was the matter of Duden's holes in one. He made twenty-two of them, including one on a par-four hole. Eight of the aces came in tournament play. No big hole-in-one prize, though.

"I got a new suit of clothes for one of them, but that's about it," he told me.

Duden, who didn't take up golf seriously until after his graduation from the University of Oregon and a stint in the military, soon became obsessed with the game. His hand-eye coordination was exceptional, and he was strictly a "feel" player. I asked him once about muscle-memory in golf, and he pooh-poohed pros who expressed the importance of it.

"I don't ever use that," he said. "I make myself do something with every shot. That helps my concentration."

Duden also was a master of trick shots, and he could bounce a ball off the clubface of an iron for seemingly endless minutes—from the front, the side and behind his back. Tiger Woods has made a lot of money in TV commercials executing the same thing, but Duden was doing it before Woods was born.

Duden, divorced in his later years, played most of his recreational golf at Glendoveer, where he also did some teaching. He was a great storyteller, too.

There was the time he was playing with three others at Waverley Country Club, in the Portland suburbs, and he and his partner were up at the turn in a tight money match. The group had played the back nine first, and the opponents put on a "pretty heavy press" going to the club's first hole, a short par-four that has a boundary road along the right side and close by the green.

"It was a foggy morning," Duden said. "I hit my drive to the right, and the ball disappeared into the fog. So I hit a provisional ball."

The foursome searched for the first ball but couldn't find it. "Our opponents were feeling pretty smug, until we discovered my ball in the cup," Duden said. "We won a bundle that day."

Two weeks later, Duden was approached by a golfing acquaintance who said, "How'd you like that hole in one the other day at Waverley?" A startled Duden said, "Where did you hear about that?"

Turns out that this fellow had been driving out that boundary road at the time of Duden's tee shot and saw his ball roll across the road and out of bounds. He stopped his car, retrieved the ball and, "just for fun," put it in the hole.

Did Duden ever tell his opponents from that day at Waverley about the new knowledge? "Not a chance," he said with a mischievous grin.

Duden was a superb shot-maker, and I got an early indication of that while watching him play in the first round of the Northwest Open at Spokane Country Club in 1964. It was a blustery day, and a par-three hole of about 165 yards was giving the players fits. Iron shots were bouncing over a rock-hard green and into the rough.

Along came Duden, who pulled out one of two four-woods that he had in his bag. I blinked in disbelief. Surely his tee shot would end up in the next county. Instead, he hit a shot that climbed into the air as if it had been struck with a nine-iron. The ball came down softly on the green and settled a few feet from the cup.

A couple holes later, he used that same four-wood for a 230-yard shot, hitting it low into a crosswind and running the ball onto the green. Then I knew that I was watching a master.

Relaxing after a 1980 tournament round, Bob Duden talks about his day on the course. *Courtesy of Pacific Northwest PGA.*

"Golf is a funny game," he once told me. "I can shoot sixty-six or seventy-five and hit the ball about the same way. Little things happen that make the difference."

Duden, of course, became famous for developing "The Dude," a croquet-style putter with a crooked shaft that allowed him to stand behind the ball and stroke the putter between his legs. He started doing well with it, and others began buying the putters and trying the unique style. He was about to have a thriving business.

Unfortunately, word got out on the PGA Tour, and some players—including Sam Snead—began putting croquet-style with various putters and some awkward-looking stances. Suddenly, the U.S. Golf Association became concerned that the style was unsightly and made it illegal to straddle the line of the ball while putting.

"That decision cost me plenty," said Duden, who turned to a similar style but stroking the ball sidesaddle from outside his legs on the right side.

Later, Snead apologized to Duden for his part in the ruling. "Bob, I'm sorry," he said. "The only reason they cut you out was because they wanted to stop me and my sidewinder (style)."

My favorite Duden story, though, came from Mike Adams, an amateur who developed his game under Duden, playing in numerous pro-amateurs with him. Adams became a good enough player to win the Oregon Coast Invitational and the Southern Oregon Amateur.

Adams wanted to show his appreciation to Duden and, in October 1992, invited him on a trip to Las Vegas to play golf and try out the casinos. However, Duden's clubs didn't arrive on their flight. He was assured they would be delivered to the hotel later that day.

"We played the Desert Inn anyway, and Bob rented some clubs and used a traditional putter," Adams said. "We were paired with two high-rollers from Texas, and Bob shot about eighty and took about forty-five putts. Afterward, the Texans bought us drinks, and one of them said, 'You know, I figure we can all lose a lot of money at the tables tonight, or we can win or lose money playing golf tomorrow against each other. It seems like we play about the same. How about $200 a hole, automatic two-down presses, $200 for KPs and $500 a nine?'"

Adams excused himself and called the hotel to see if Duden's clubs had arrived. They had. He returned to the table and privately told Duden that his clubs were in his room at the hotel and that he would cover the bets.

"Well, Duden birdied the first three holes, I birdied the fourth, Duden birdied the fifth and got a KP and I birdied the sixth," Adams said. "We took those Texas boys for $3,600 that day."

Afterward, the Texans lauded Duden's game and wondered if he had considered turning pro. One of them asked him if he ever had won a tournament. Seldom without a sense of humor, Duden replied, "Well, a long time ago, I won the Blind Bogey in Walla Walla, Washington."

When he died at seventy-four, Duden was in the front seat of his car in his driveway. Naturally, he was on his way to a golf course.

Chapter 2

THE LIFETIME AMATEURS

K ent Myers said that he yearned to play on the amateur Hudson Cup team in his early years as a competitive golfer in Oregon.

"I had a pretty good record, too, but it seemed that I just got ignored," he said. "I grew up as a public-course golfer (at Salem Golf Club), and I guess I wasn't on anybody's list."

That all changed in 1965 when Myers, who didn't start playing golf until his late teens, won his first of four Oregon Amateur titles and did it in such dramatic fashion that a Hudson Cup invitation was a foregone conclusion. The retired school administrator from Lake Oswego looks back on that tournament at Portland Golf Club as a springboard to his later success. Included in this success have been nineteen appearances as a Hudson Cup amateur team player against teams of the Pacific Northwest's top club pros and eighteen times as the amateur team captain.

"Once I got my foot in the door, I was in for the long haul," he said with a smile.

Mary Budke also got her start on an Oregon public course, Riverwood in Dundee, when she was eight. Guy Hupe, the Riverwood pro, gave her early instruction. She became so hooked on the game that she even dug herself a sand bunker in the backyard of the family home in Dayton.

"I didn't get to use that bunker much," Budke said. "The cats took it over."

Budke, who won the U.S. Women's Amateur in 1972, beating Cynthia Hill five and four in the final at St. Louis Country Club, also had a springboard moment in the Oregon Amateur, hers in the 1970 tournament in a match that

Kent Myers uses his optional and unique putting style, holding the putter behind his back and extending the shaft between his legs. He used the style effectively in some of his biggest amateur tournament wins. *Courtesy of Pacific Northwest GA.*

she lost. She was sixteen when she faced Cathy Gaughan at Gaughan's home Eugene Country Club in the thirty-six-hole final. Gaughan was the two-time defending titlist and was on a hot streak. A week earlier, she had won the National Women's Collegiate Championship while playing for Arizona State.

Gaughan, later to play on the LPGA Tour as Cathy Mant and later still to become women's golf coach at Georgia State University, prevailed one-up by winning the final four holes after Budke, playing superbly, built as much as a five-up lead.

"I was disappointed that I lost, but the experience was almost all positive," said Budke, who retired as an emergency medicine physician in Eugene late in 2010 and moved to Palm Springs, California. "I learned a lot from that match that helped me later on. Besides, Cathy and I were great friends. I even stayed at the Gaughan family home that week."

Such is the way Myers and Budke made their moves, so to speak, away from the temptation to turn pro and toward exceptional careers as lifetime amateur golfers.

Myers went into the 1965 Oregon Amateur as anything but a favorite, and his optimism wavered when he had to replace a broken shaft in his driver the day before the tournament.

"I never did get the feel of the driver that week," he said. "I just kept snap-hooking it, and my ball ended up in some bad places."

But that just gave the 140-pound Myers the chance to show off his fiery competitiveness and creativity and to demonstrate his scrambling ability and putting prowess. He was down in every match but one and just kept rallying from the brink of defeat.

In the second round, he was even with John Hedlund on the final hole, a par-five of 513 yards, and hooked his second shot into fir trees about 75 yards short of the green. He ran a low shot from there through limbs and sank a thirty-five-foot birdie putt to win one-up. "Like playing out of a daylight basement," he jokingly said of his predicament in the trees.

In the quarterfinals, he had to go to the nineteenth hole to eliminate three-time Amateur champion Bob Atkinson of the host club. He did it by blasting from a bunker at the extra hole to within eight feet and sinking the par putt. That became good enough when Atkinson missed a shorter par putt.

In the thirty-six-hole semifinals, Myers faced Bruce Cudd, a former Walker Cup golfer who later would play briefly on the PGA Tour. Cudd seemed in complete control with a three-up lead heading to the twenty-eighth hole. That was especially true after Myers pushed his second shot from the left rough on the par-five hole, and the ball ended up far right—partially behind a bush and with a tree and bunker between it and the green.

Somehow, Myers chipped a four-iron shot that barely cleared the bush, went under an overhanging limb, bounced over the bunker and stopped ten feet from the cup. Then, he turned to what he called his "alternate putting stroke," holding the putter behind his back with the shaft extending down between his legs. He sank the birdie putt to win the hole. Unnerved, Cudd hit the ball out of play on the next two holes to lose the rest of his lead. Myers eventually won one-up.

Myers developed the unusual putting style while in the army in Texas. Excluded from fellow soldiers' putting contests because he was winning too much of the money, he practiced the behind-the-back style until it felt comfortable. Then he asked if he could rejoin the contests if he used his unorthodox stroke. He was accepted and soon resumed his money-winning ways.

Finally, in the thirty-six-hole final, Myers again had to go into an escape-artist mode against Portland State University golfer Bob Smith. Four-down at one point and still one-down going to the thirty-fifth hole, a par-three, he had to come out of a bunker and make a par putt of six feet for a halve after Smith missed a ten-foot birdie try. Then he won the thirty-sixth hole with a par, again coming out of trees, to force a playoff. He won the playoff with a forty-foot birdie at the thirty-seventh.

Mary Budke grimaces as she hits a shot in a 1972 tournament, the year that she won the U.S. Women's Amateur. *Courtesy of Pacific Northwest GA.*

Budke, who had caddied for Gaughan the year before in the latter's title-match win in the Amateur over Molly Cronin, got off to a quick start and was five-up after nine holes. She was two-up after eighteen but then increased her lead back to three-up with a two-under-par thirty-three on the afternoon round's front nine. She still was three-up with four holes to play before her game cracked.

"One of the things I learned that day was that I needed to be able to fade the ball when the shot called for it," Budke said. "I was a draw player in those days, and I kind of hated Eugene's back nine, which called for a fade on so many holes."

Gaughan had her lone lead of the day after winning the thirty-sixth hole. "It was the toughest match I've ever been in," she said at the time. The women's final offered so much drama for spectators that it upstaged Mike Davis, a two-time

Pacific Coast Amateur champion, as he defeated Mike Alley six and five for the men's title.

Looking back to his prime golfing years, Myers said, "I always lived on the edge." In addition to his four Oregon Amateur titles (the others in 1972, 1981 and 1983), he won the Pacific Northwest Golf Association Senior Amateur in 1992 and the PNGA Master-Forty title in 1994. Earlier, at Willamette University in Salem, he won the Northwest Conference championship. He also qualified for the 1956 U.S. Open in Rochester, New York, missing the cut.

In 1987, when he was fifty-five, he was runner-up in the Pacific Northwest Amateur at Washington's Tacoma Country and Golf Club. Of the eight quarterfinalists that year, the next oldest was twenty-three. "I got called 'the old man' a lot that week," he said.

Myers, who was inducted into the Pacific Northwest Golf Hall of Fame in 2001, has had eleven holes in one and began shooting his age when he was sixty-six. He had a seventy-five one day in 2011, when he was seventy-nine.

In addition to her U.S. Women's Amateur title, Budke won the Oregon Amateur a record eight times (1971–74 and 1976–79), won the Pacific Northwest Women's Amateur in 1976, took three straight championships in the Oregon Junior Girls Amateur, was titlist twice in the Pacific Northwest Junior Girls Amateur and won the inaugural Oregon High School Girls Tournament title in 1971 after previously competing with the boys.

She also earned all-American honors at Oregon State University and had a third-place finish in the National Women's Collegiate tournament in 1974. She was selected for some halls of fame and was named winner of the Bill Hayward Award as Oregon's top amateur athlete in 1972.

Mary Budke, who claimed a record eight Oregon Women's Amateur titles in her career, watches the result of her shot in 1977 tournament action. *Courtesy of Pacific Northwest GA.*

Budke, who made four of her five holes in one in tournament play, qualified for the U.S. Women's Open in 1974 and tied for forty-second. She played on the U.S. Curtis Cup team the same year, winning two of three matches. In 2002, she was the winning captain when the United States won the Curtis Cup matches over the Great Britain/Ireland team 11-7 at Pittsburgh, Pennsylvania.

Despite their seeming potential, neither Myers nor Budke gave serious consideration to turning pro.

"I think I could have been a middle-of-the pack player on the LPGA Tour but not one of the top players, and that wouldn't have been good enough to satisfy me," Budke said. "Besides, I didn't like the idea of playing that much golf."

So, with no regrets, Myers and Budke became lifetime amateurs. The late Bobby Jones, king of the lifetime amateurs and a co-founder of Augusta National Golf Club, undoubtedly would have been impressed.

Chapter 3

ARNIE'S OPEN COLLAPSE

The last twosome in the 1966 U.S. Open's final round was making the nine-hole turn at the Olympic Club, and there was a massive exodus of golf writers from the course to the tournament's media center. Seemingly, it was time to get an early start on stories.

One cynical scribe said to no one in particular, "This was a fine tournament for three days. Now it's a shambles."

Arnold Palmer was in the midst of one of his magical charges that had produced a seven-shot lead over playing companion Billy Casper.

One of the writers to depart was my friend Joe Much, later to become executive director of the National Golf Foundation but then sports editor of the *Capital Journal* in Salem, Oregon. He waited for me to join him. But this was my first Open as golf writer for the *Oregonian*, and I wasn't about to spend that final nine in the media center.

"I don't care if Arnie wins by twenty strokes, I'm going to watch," I told Much. He laughed and waved at me as I headed for the tenth hole.

Thus is how I came to see in person what frequently has been described as the greatest collapse in Open history or, looking at it in another way, the greatest comeback.

Palmer was pumped. He later would admit that, heading to that final nine, he was more focused on breaking Ben Hogan's Open record of 276 than he was on worrying about his pursuers at the club in the San Francisco suburbs. He just needed a one-over-par thirty-six on the back nine to break the mark.

Walking down the tenth fairway, I saw the two players converse briefly. Casper was expressing concern about holding off budding star Jack Nicklaus for second place. "Don't worry, Bill, you'll finish second," Palmer admitted to saying, words that would come back to haunt him for years to come.

As I strolled along beside the tenth fairway, I marveled at how the tournament had come down to this—a head-to-head showdown of two of the game's brightest stars. My stories with "local angles" on first-round leader Al Mengert, a club pro from Tacoma, Washington, and Oregon club pro Jim Petersen were history. After his opening sixty-seven, Mengert had faded, eventually to tie for twenty-sixth place. Petersen, after a contending seventy-two in the first round, had missed the cut with a second-round eighty.

Palmer's lead still was a comfortable six strokes with six holes to play when I introduced myself to Jim Murray, popular and sometimes controversial columnist of the *Los Angeles Times*. We began walking together. He seemed friendly, and I thought we were hitting it off in grand style.

Then it happened. Palmer was too greedy, going for pins on two par-threes—the thirteenth and fifteenth—and made bogeys on each, while Casper had a par at the thirteenth and a birdie at the fifteenth on a twenty-foot putt. Suddenly, the lead was down to three with three holes to play.

"After the fifteenth, that's when I quit playing for second place," Casper would say later.

While all this was going on, Murray's disposition gradually changed. He became edgy and less inclined to converse.

Meanwhile, I had difficulty fathoming what I was seeing, especially after Palmer's drive at the 604-yard sixteenth hooked wildly into a tree, the ball dropping less than 120 yards from the tee. Spectators, most of them Palmer supporters, were stunned. So was I as I watched Arnie pull out a three-iron for his next shot from rough that came up over his ankles. The ball slithered across the fairway, advancing barely seventy-five yards and into more rough.

While Palmer was unraveling, Casper played two conservative shots down the fairway and then fired a five-iron to within fifteen feet of the cup. Palmer, finally reaching a greenside bunker in four, made a courageous bogey by blasting out and sinking a four-foot putt. But his plight had become desperate after Casper sank his birdie putt to pull within one stroke of the lead.

When Casper made that birdie, I blurted, "What a great putt!"

A smiling Arnold Palmer, shown here at the Inaugural Fred Meyer Challenge in 1986, says one of his biggest career disappointments was his loss in the 1966 U.S. Open. *Photo by Michael Lloyd/Oregonian.*

"Oh, shut up," Murray said, and he walked away in a huff. He never spoke to me again that weekend, even though our seats were just one row apart in the media center.

As I headed to the seventeenth hole, I saw an amusing sight of more than one hundred press representatives hustling from the media center to watch play on the last two holes. Among them was Joe Much, who grinned as he came up to me and said, "OK, so you were right to stay out here. I don't want to hear any more about it."

Several writers asked me for details about the various back nine happenings. I shared them as we moved toward the seventeenth green, where the last stroke of Palmer's lead would evaporate when he left a seven-foot par putt a couple inches short.

Palmer then nursed in a ticklish side-hill putt of five feet at the 337-yard eighteenth for a par that gave him a playoff chance when Casper also made a par. The two had tied at a 2-under-par 278.

"I just hit a few bad shots," Palmer said during his news conference. "That's about the only explanation."

Casper's analysis seemed more revealing. He said, "This is a demanding course, which you can't charge too much. You have to romance it a little bit, and that's what I tried to do."

Palmer later admitted that he became annoyed on the back nine by Casper's "play it safe" game, and that might have contributed to his downfall.

The media center was a mess that evening. Those were the days of typewriters and Western Union operators, and the floor was covered with wads of typing paper as writers threw away story starts that had become inappropriate. Murray had several wads in his vicinity.

The eighteen-hole playoff the next day was more of the same, but without the final round's drama. Casper shot a sixty-nine with a thirty-four on the back nine to claim the championship. Palmer, who led early, sagged to forty on the back for a seventy-three.

While Palmer did blow the championship, I chose to emphasize the importance of Casper's brilliant thirty-two on the closing round's final nine. After all, if a guy has a seven-shot lead with nine holes to go in a U.S. Open and shoots a thirty-nine, it doesn't figure that he would lose.

In a sidelight, there was the U.S. Golf Association's rule at the time that players had to use caddies made available by the host club. I knew two of them quite well—Mike Reasor from Seattle and Jim McNeeley, who played golf at Astoria Golf and Country Club on the Oregon Coast. Gene "Bunny" Mason, a Portland club pro and also an officer of the PGA, made the arrangements for them to be in the caddie pool.

"I was sitting next to Mike in the caddie room when they were drawing for players," McNeeley recalled. "They drew for him first, and he got Palmer. Then they drew for me, and I got Gene Bone."

Bone made the cut, tied for thirty-sixth and earned $790. "He paid me $90 and gave me bunch of Spalding golf balls," McNeeley said. Reasor, who died unexpectedly in 2002 between rounds of a Northwest regional tournament, was paid more than $1,000 as Palmer earned $14,000 for second place.

Reasor also became a valuable news source for me that week. For instance, he described this scene late on Sunday night after Casper and Palmer had ended in the tie.

"I was in my motel room and feeling miserable," he said. "I kept thinking that there should have been some way that I could have helped save him a stroke on that final nine. The phone rang. It was Palmer, and he apologized to me for not winning. I was on my knees with tears in my eyes. I couldn't believe, knowing how he felt, that he would take the time to call me."

Murray's reaction puzzled me for years. After his death, I had a chance to talk to his widow, Linda McCoy-Murray, about what had happened that day long ago.

"I remember Jim talking about walking the last nine holes with Arnold," she said. "He said he felt as if he had been watching a complicated suicide."

She added, "Jim and Arnold had a deep friendship. Jim called him 'Arnold America.'"

McCoy-Murray also told me a story about Murray watching Palmer during a round of a Los Angeles Open at Riviera Country Club. Palmer pulled a drive into an area of pop cans and other debris. The lie was awful.

While contemplating his next shot, he spotted Murray, also a big admirer of Ben Hogan, standing nearby and said, "What would your idol Hogan do in this situation?"

"Hogan would never be in this situation," Murray replied.

Finally, I had a better understanding of why Murray had told me to "shut up" that day at the Olympic Club.

Chapter 4

BLUNDER IN A BUNKER

W hen I covered the 1966 U.S. Open at the Olympic Club, I thought I had witnessed golf's most significant blowup of all time. It just didn't make sense that there could be anything to rival Arnold Palmer frittering away a seven-shot lead with nine holes to play and Billy Casper charging to a final-nine thirty-two to catch him and force a playoff. Casper then won the playoff the next day, sixty-nine to seventy-three.

So there was no way I could have anticipated that, in 1969, I would cover an even more astounding reversal of fortunes. It came in Oregon at the scenic, tree-lined Portland Golf Club, and it came with much larger financial rewards on the line.

It was the Alcan Golfer of the Year Championship, an international tournament with a select field of twenty-four of some of the world's finest players. Included were the likes of Casper, Lee Trevino, Frank Beard, Gene Littler, Lou Graham, Dan Sikes, Gay Brewer, David Graham, Bernard Gallacher, Christy O'Connor and Kel Nagle.

The media attention was modest, with fewer than fifty representatives. The attention-grabber was that the winner would earn $55,000, the game's largest payoff at the time. For comparison, Casper got a check for $26,500 for his 1966 Open win.

Then lightning struck a second time for Casper. Just like at the Olympic Club, he played for second place in the final round and ended up with the top prize. But that's getting ahead of the story.

Despite the big purse, the players were anything but uptight as they participated in a pro-amateur and a pre-tournament clinic. At the clinic, a

Lee Trevino speaks to fans at Portland Golf Club after collapsing on the last three holes and losing to Billy Casper in the 1969 Alcan Golfer of the Year Championship. *Courtesy of Portland Golf Club.*

fan asked Trevino, the 1968 U.S. Open champion, to demonstrate how he could hit a ball with a pop bottle, a feat for which he had gained considerable fame. He got a bottle from a spectator and, consecutively, threw three balls into the air. He hit one high, one low and one in between. All three traveled between eighty and one hundred yards.

Meanwhile, Casper lamented his need for practice because "I haven't been playing much lately." But actually, he had been on a prolonged hot streak, winning six times in 1968 and claiming titles in the Bob Hope Desert Classic and the Western Open in 1969.

And as the pro-amateur concluded, there was little doubt that Trevino and Casper were the favorites to contend for the title and that $55,000 prize. It wasn't lost on the contestants that there was a huge drop-off to $15,000 for second place.

Sikes and Graham shared the first-round lead with 69, while Trevino and Casper were in a five-way tie for third with 70. But by the end of the second round, Trevino had rushed into the lead with a 67 and 137, and Casper was tied for second with a 68 and 138.

In a sidelight, Nagle was completely out of contention after that second round. His scorecard showed a 35, his front-nine score, in the space reserved for his ninth-hole total. He didn't catch the mistake before signing and turning in his scorecard and had to take the 35, instead of the four that he made. He wound up with an eighteen-hole total of 105.

"I came a long ways to make a stupid mistake like that," said the Australian, who stuck around for closing rounds of seventy-three and seventy-six to collect last-place money of $2,000.

Trevino kept his lead with a third-round 69 for a 10-under 206, and Casper was alone in second after a 70 for 208. The stage was set. The only disappointment was that, in the pairings format at the time, the two heavyweights would not be paired together for the final round, Casper going off in the next-to-last twosome, just in front of Trevino.

Writing about golf is different from writing about most sports. To see as much action as possible, you must walk the course with the players. In the final round, I started out following Trevino, the leader, and the "Merry Mex" gave me no reason to go elsewhere—at least until the final minutes of the round. He surged to five birdies in six holes through the tenth for a five-shot lead.

His followers, a few wearing Mexican sombreros, were whooping it up. And as Casper admitted later, "I thought Lee had come and gone with the tournament."

Trevino, who made his sixth birdie of the day at the thirteenth, lost a stroke with a three-putt bogey at the fourteenth. Unperturbed, he hit a sensational four-wood shot from 240 yards to within ten feet of the cup at the par-five fifteenth. When he sank the eagle putt, he danced around the green and chatted it up with spectators.

Billy Casper (second from right) is surrounded by well-wishers as he watches Lee Trevino miss a birdie putt at the final hole, clinching the title for Casper in the 1969 Alcan Golfer of the Year Championship. *Courtesy of Portland Golf Club.*

I was caught up in the excitement myself at the spectacular round I was witnessing. I already was thinking up possible leads for my story

Despite making a birdie at the fifteenth, Casper found himself six shots behind as he played the sixteenth. He was intent on securing second place, just as he had been three years earlier against Palmer.

Then it happened. Casper's birdie at the sixteenth reduced Trevino's lead to five. Trevino pulled his drive at the sixteenth—a dogleg left par-four, behind a tree—and had to chip out. The resulting bogey cut his lead to four.

Casper made a seven-foot birdie at the simple-seeming 145-yard seventeenth, and Trevino followed by making a complete mess of the seventeenth. The pin was placed near the front of the green, behind a deep, menacing bunker. Trevino went with a nine-iron. It wasn't enough club. His ball caught the lip of the bunker and buried, about a foot short of being a perfect shot.

Gasps came from the gallery when Trevino failed to get the ball out of the sand with his next shot. On top of that, the ball rolled back into one of his footprints, leaving him an even more hazardous lie. He then managed to escape from the bunker, but his ball slithered to the right, thirty feet from the pin. Unnerved, he three-putted for a triple-bogey.

Suddenly, Trevino's lead was gone, and when he heard a roar up ahead at the green of the uphill, 560-yard eighteenth, he feared the worst. Casper, after another radar-like iron shot, had made his fourth consecutive birdie to take a one-shot lead.

After a good drive at eighteen, Trevino spotted me walking inside the gallery ropes on the right side of the fairway. He ambled over, a frown blanketing his usually jovial face.

"How does it stand?" he asked. I think he knew but was hoping for good news. I told him he was one behind. He grimaced and said, "I'm so upset, I can't even think."

Then, after Trevino hit a good second shot to within eighty yards of the green, I quickly moved up ahead and spotted Casper sitting in a roped-off area of bleachers behind the green. He was staring at an IBM electronic scoreboard that was reporting Trevino's triple-bogey.

"What does it mean?" Casper asked. Told that he had a one-stroke lead, he said, "I just can't believe it."

Trevino got his third shot at eighteen to within fifteen feet, but his curling birdie putt, which would have forced a playoff, slid below the cup. His collapse was complete.

Unbelievably, Casper had beaten Trevino by 7 strokes on the last three holes, shooting a 6-under-par 66 for a 14-under 274 finish. Trevino, despite his late flameout, had a 69 for 275.

Asked to compare his comeback to the one he made against Palmer in the U.S. Open, Casper replied, "It was even more fantastic. There, I could see it coming. Here, it was thrown at me blindside."

Trevino called his club selection at the seventeenth a "cardinal sin" before heading for the airport and a flight to Singapore for the World Cup.

In 1987, Trevino returned to Portland Golf Club to play in Peter Jacobsen's Fred Meyer Challenge. For the pro-amateur, he was paired to start at the seventeenth hole in the event's shotgun format.

"This is cold-blooded," he said with a grin as he strolled to the tee. He hit the green with an eight-iron but three-putted for a bogey. The hole still had his number. Then he noticed that the bunker in front of the seventeenth had been remodeled, taking away its abrupt lip and modifying its depth.

"You can almost putt a ball out of there now," he said. "I bet the members figured, if Lee Trevino can't get out of that bunker, we can't either, and decided to fill it up."

Chapter 5

MEMORIES OF "SLAMMIN' SAM"

Sam Snead was in one of his famed storytelling moods on that spring day of 1985, and he seemed to relish talking about his first of three victories in the PGA Championship in 1942.

"It was just before I was inducted into the navy," he said. "I had to talk a guy into delaying my induction a week in order for me to play. I told him I had a chance to win $2,000. He turned out to be the right guy because he arranged for me to be inducted on Monday, the day after the tournament [at Atlantic City, New Jersey]."

Snead then survived the demanding rigors of match play (the PGA's format at the time), beating Jim Turnesa two and one in the final.

"After the tournament, I gave the guy in the induction office a set of golf clubs and some balls," Snead said. "He asked me if I wanted a two-week pass."

Snead was in the Portland area on this occasion for a pair of exhibitions, one at the Fairway Village course in nearby Vancouver, Washington. So, naturally, he recalled also winning his first tournament after his navy tour of duty. It was in the Portland Open at Portland Golf Club in the fall of 1944.

"That might have been the wettest tournament I ever played in," he said. "It was so bad that water came up over your shoes and ran down into them. But I didn't mind. I was just itching to play after all that time in the navy."

Snead also played at Portland Golf Club in the 1946 PGA Championship and in the 1947 Ryder Cup matches in which he had a 2-0 record as the United States, with Ben Hogan as captain, won easily, 11-1.

Asked about his golfing longevity, Snead talked about exercising and "staying away from alcohol." That led to another story.

"It was the 1955 Miami Open, and I was tied with Tommy Bolt after seventy-two holes," he said. "I thought we were going to have an eighteen-hole playoff the next day, so I had a beer. The next thing I know they are telling me that it is a sudden-death playoff and that I'm on the tee."

Snead said he was dizzy as he teed off, and he pushed his ball deep into pine trees. "You have to remember that I drank hardly at all," he said. "One beer really affected me." By the time he reached his ball, though, his head had cleared, and he hit a miraculous two-iron shot that faded about seventy yards around trees and onto the green. He won the playoff with a par.

"Tommy was kind of upset," a smiling Snead said. "He figured there was no way I could have gotten out of those trees like that. He said someone in the gallery must have moved my ball into an open area."

Many of the reports of things Snead supposedly said simply weren't true. "But I haven't objected because most of them I would have said if I had thought of it," he said.

A classic comment that he confirmed making was one before he played in his first British Open, in 1946 at St. Andrews. He took his first look at the barren links and said, "Where's the golf course?"

Then there was the time that a writer, sympathizing with Sam, said, "It's too bad there never was a U.S. Open with your name on it." Snead replied, "Oh, there were probably a few, but I erased it every time."

Over the years, I had a few more chances to visit with the golfer frequently called "Slammin' Sam." He told me he didn't particularly like that nickname, and he definitely didn't like to be called "Sammy."

At the inaugural Fred Meyer Challenge in 1986, an unofficial event with Peter Jacobsen as host, Snead was on hand to play an exhibition round with Chi Chi Rodriguez at Portland GC. In an interview session, he was asked to name the game's best players of all time.

"[Jack] Nicklaus was the best, especially for a stretch of about twelve years, and he was a great putter," he said. "For second best, it's a tossup between [Byron] Nelson and Hogan. Nelson was a better driver and hit long irons better. Hogan was better around the greens and with putting."

Modestly, he didn't mention himself. And, of course, that was long before Tiger Woods arrived on the tour scene.

I once asked Snead about the confusion over his official number of PGA Tour victories, a hot button to him. After the PGA Tour became a new organization and took over direction of the tour from PGA of America, several of Snead's victories were thrown out as not being significant enough. He eventually was credited with eighty-one, still the all-time leading number. He won seven majors.

"I won a lot more tournaments [than eighty-one], but they won't count them all," he said. For instance, he said he had a difficult time understanding why none of his four victories in the Bing Crosby Clambake (later renamed the AT&T Pebble Beach Pro-Amateur) was counted while other players' wins in the event were counted.

Another time, Snead told me he thought the golf cup size should be increased to six inches from its regulation four-and-one-fourth inches.

"Think about it," he said. "Here you have a game where a two-inch putt counts the same as a three-hundred-yard drive. Now isn't that ridiculous? I like the idea of a bigger cup to make putting less important. A lot of older players give up the game because they get so frustrated with their putting. That's too bad."

Slow play sometimes was as painful to him as a thorn in his index finger. He occasionally lost his cool about it, and one of those times came in the 1955 Western Open at Portland Golf Club. He was playing with Oregon club pro Bob McKendrick in the group behind that of Cary Middlecoff. Snead felt that Middlecoff was dawdling. At the tenth hole, Snead walked ahead from his ball in the fairway to the green where Middlecoff was preparing to putt.

"Hit the ball or get off the green!" Snead shouted.

Slow or not, Middlecoff went on to win that tournament, shooting a nine-under-par sixty-three in the final round, including a six-under twenty-nine on the front nine.

Gene "Bunny" Mason, a longtime club pro in Oregon and also a course designer before his death in 2010, once said of Snead, "He had a classic swing, and his secret was rhythm. He was a marvelous athlete. His flexibility, even when he was older, was amazing. I remember when [amateur] Frank Stranahan challenged him to a one-hundred-yard race when Sam was in his forties, and Stranahan was in his late twenties. Sam beat him."

Snead, known for being crude at times and for telling off-color jokes, also took delight in "money games" any time he could line them up. If he could, he wasn't averse to tilting the odds in his favor, either.

On his visit to Vancouver, he ended up in a skins game with Oregon pros Jerry Mowlds, Bob Duden and Pat Fitzsimons. "Sam was the only one not to win a skin," Mowlds said. "He didn't like that a bit."

Sam was a frequent participant and a fan favorite in the Par-Three Contest prelude to the Masters in the 1990s while being on hand to hit an honorary tee shot to open the tournament. In 1994, in the Par-Three Contest, I saw him hit a tee shot over a pond to within two feet of the cup at the ninth hole. Spectators roared. They roared again when he sank the birdie putt.

I last saw Snead in 1997 at the Masters when he was having health problems and was accompanied on the trip by his son, Jack.

"He can't see his golf ball in flight anymore, but he can see the ball on the ground in front of him," Jack said. "And if you give him a distance, say 127 yards, he can hit a shot that distance by feel. He still can play pretty well."

Snead came to Augusta for the last time in 2002. He hit the last golf shot of his life there, a pushed drive into spectators lining the first fairway. Six weeks later, on May 23, four days before he would have turned ninety, he died at his home near Hot Springs, Virginia.

Golf had lost one of its finest players and one of its most unforgettable characters.

Of course, as Mowlds pointed out, he can't be forgotten. "Not with so many future players watching him on tape, that perfect grip, that amazing tempo," Mowlds said.

Chapter 6

EXCITING CHARGE AT RIVIERA

Peter Jacobsen crouched over an eight-foot birdie putt at Riviera Country Club's taxing eighteenth hole. It was his final hole of the second round of the 1983 PGA Championship, and a birdie would give the Portland golfer a 69 for the round and a 142 total for thirty-six holes.

"It was a fairly easy putt with a slight right-to-left break," he said.

But just as Jacobsen started his stroke, the words "Welcome to Riviera Country Club" came from an ESPN tower above the eighteenth green. Jacobsen flinched noticeably, and his putt missed badly.

Seething, he tapped in for his par and a 70 for 143. Then he glowered at the tower. "Do you mind being quiet?" he shouted.

After signing his scorecard, Jacobsen headed straight for the tower, where TV announcer Jim Simpson had been rehearsing for his opening the next day. Jacobsen, not one to lose his cool often, definitely lost it momentarily on this day.

He pushed past a security guard and climbed up to the booth to seek out Simpson. A woman, who claimed to be in charge, stopped him.

She told him the booth was soundproof, and he told her she was "dead wrong." She told him they "didn't mean to do it," and Jacobsen responded by telling her "that won't cut it." Then he let Simpson know how he felt.

Later, after calming down, Jacobsen said, "Those people are going to learn not to fool around with me. All they care about are five or six guys—Jack Nicklaus, Arnold Palmer, Gary Player, Lee Trevino, Tom Watson, people like that. I've had it with the TV attitude. They are all hush-hush for the big names, but they just ignore the rest of us and what we're doing."

Such was one of my storylines for a major championship that turned into one of my most exciting as a golf writer. And it just got more exciting after that at the storied course in Pacific Palisades, California.

Already, I had a great local angle as John Fought, another Portland player and a former U.S. Amateur champion, was battling for the lead. Rounds of 67 and 69 had him in fourth place at 6-under-par 136, 5 shots behind streaking Hal Sutton, who was at 131, a PGA tournament record for the first thirty-six holes.

"I've never played any better for two rounds here, and I've done well in the Los Angeles Open here," Fought said. "Now it just is a matter of getting myself into position and keeping my concentration."

Bob Gilder, still another Oregonian, also had a 69 while playing in Fought's threesome and was at 140. I had a busy but potentially fun weekend looming ahead.

Fought continued to hang in there in the third round, shooting a 71 on a day when scoring went up. At 207, he was in third place behind Sutton (203) and Ben Crenshaw (205). I looked ahead to a tense final round when Fought would be paired with Sutton and Crenshaw in the final threesome.

"I'm not too worried about Hal," Fought said, startling a gathering of media. "I know he might run away and hide from us, but I don't expect that to happen. If I can just play my game and get a little under, I'll have a chance to win."

Meanwhile, out of the spotlight, Jacobsen managed a 68 for 211 and a tie for fifteenth place. His round included a ball hooked out of bounds at the par-five first hole. He minimized the damage by making a birdie with his second ball to save a bogey.

Since Gilder fell out of the picture with a seventy-six, I was left for Sunday's closing round with special interest in a title contender (Fought) and a player hoping to crack the top ten with a strong round (Jacobsen).

At the start of that final round, Sutton appeared to all but put victory away, shaking off the challenges of Fought and Crenshaw and briefly moving to thirteen under par and five shots in front. Through eight holes, Fought was one under par for the round and had lost ground to the leader.

Then, suddenly, things got a lot more interesting. Nicklaus began clawing from behind, and I was stunned when I saw a leaderboard on the eighth hole that showed that Jacobsen was putting up red numbers in bunches.

Peter Jacobsen, shown lining up a putt in a 1990 event, had one of his finest rounds when he charged into a third-place finish in the 1983 PGA Championship at Riviera Country Club near Los Angeles. *Courtesy of Peter Jacobsen Sports.*

I was amused when I heard a spectator say, "Who is this guy Jacobsen? What does he look like?"

Jacobsen had shot a thirty-one on the front nine, and he was seven under par for the day through twelve holes after making his fourth consecutive birdie. Suddenly, he was very much in the hunt at nine under for the tournament, and I rushed from the final threesome to pick up his group.

I got there just in time to see him drive into the rough and make a bogey at the thirteenth, but he didn't seem distressed. He looked calm and coldly determined heading to the fourteenth tee.

Among the gallery following Jacobsen's group, I spotted actor Jack Lemmon, a close friend of Jacobsen and his annual partner in the Pebble Beach National Pro-Amateur, then popularly known as the Crosby Clambake. I introduced myself and asked Lemmon if I could walk with him. "Sure, but I'm pretty nervous about what's going on here," he said with a smile.

I soon saw what he meant. As Jacobsen made a string of pars, Lemmon frequently looked like a nervous wreck. He got particularly tense when Jacobsen pulled his drive into rough at the 578-yard seventeenth. We were watching from the opposite side of the fairway when Jacobsen rifled a long iron out of trouble and into good position for a short third shot on the par-five hole.

"That's absolutely perfect out of that crap," Lemmon shouted as Jacobsen's ball sailed through the air. The outburst drew laughter from nearby fans.

Jacobsen made a birdie on the hole to get back to nine under and was within a shot of the lead as Sutton had faded to ten under. Nicklaus also was at nine under.

The title bid for Jacobsen then came to a disappointing end when he hit an errant drive into trees, leading to a bogey at the eighteenth. Still, he had shot 65, best round of the day, and claimed third place at 276. Sutton, making pars on the last four holes, won with 274, shooting a final-round 71. Nicklaus claimed runner-up honors with a 66 and 275.

Jacobsen, who took just twenty-seven putts in his final round, said he never checked a leaderboard on the back nine. "My caddie [Mike Cowan] is a good one, and he knows to keep me informed if there is something I should know," he said.

I later talked to Lemmon about Jacobsen and their friendship.

"He is like a son to me," he said. "To watch that gorgeous round brought tears to my eyes. It gave me a hernia in my heart. It was like watching [Lawrence] Olivier give a peak performance."

As it turned out, Jacobsen's third-place finish equaled the best he would have in one of golf's majors. He also finished third in the 1986 PGA. Later, he won a pair of majors on the Champions Tour—the 2004 U.S. Senior Open and 2005 Senior Players Championship.

Almost lost in the dramatic finish at Riviera was Fought's solid 71, good for 278 and fifth place. That meant that I had two players from my state in the top five of a major championship. I looked forward to getting started on my stories.

At the same time, I couldn't help but play the "what if" game. What if Simpson's voice from the tower hadn't interrupted Jacobsen's putting stroke in the second round, and what if Jacobsen hadn't hit that drive out of bounds to start his third round?

Years later, I had some amusing memories of 1983 at Riviera when Jacobsen became an active TV analyst for PGA Tour events. So far as I know, he never rehearsed lines while a player was putting nearby.

Chapter 7

GILDER TO THE RESCUE

B ob Gilder's drive off the eighteenth tee was hooked badly, and he grimaced as he watched the errant shot's trajectory. The ball appeared to come down in a rough-surrounded bunker, the last place he wanted it to be at this crucial moment.

It was the final day of the 1983 Ryder Cup matches at the PGA National Golf Club in Palm Beach Gardens, Florida, and Gilder and his United States teammates were struggling to stave off a spirited challenge from the Europeans.

Gilder, one-up on Gordon Brand going to the par-five eighteenth, found his ball in an even worse position than he anticipated. Instead of being in the bunker, it was lodged deep in eight-inch rough leading down to the sand. With the stance he would have had to take, he had no chance to advance it forward. He slumped momentarily and then slashed a sand wedge shot out sideways into the fairway.

It appeared that Brand likely would win the hole, earn a halve in the match and give his side a valuable half point in the hotly contested team battle.

That's when Gilder, a quiet man with a no-nonsense approach on a golf course, came up with a career-enhancing shot. From about 245 yards, with water on the right side and with United States captain, Jack Nicklaus, watching from a hillside left of the fairway, he hit a fairway wood that tracked laser-like to the edge of the green. It was a relatively easy up-and-down from there for a par, and when an unnerved Brand chipped poorly and made a bogey, Gilder had a two-up victory and a crucial point for his team.

Later, Lanny Wadkins was one-down to Jose Maria Canizares on the eighteenth before hitting a sensational wedge shot from sixty yards to barely more than a foot from the cup. His birdie won him the hole and earned him a match-deciding halve. Spectators roared, and a relieved Nicklaus bent down and kissed Wadkins's divot mark.

The United States had squeezed by 14 1/2 to 13 1/2, and Wadkins got most of the post-match attention. Much also was made of a 240-yard shot with a three-wood by European Seve Ballesteros from the same bunker that had been such an obstacle for Gilder. Ballesteros's shot, a perfectly executed fade from the sand, found the green and led him to a tie with Fuzzy Zoeller.

"The finest shot I've ever seen," Nicklaus said of Ballesteros's shot.

Still, I thought Gilder deserved equal praise for his magical recovery at eighteen. With the pressure extreme, he hit a shot that conjured up memories of the three-wood shot from 251 yards that he sank for a double-eagle on his way to victory at the 1982 Westchester Classic.

"This one wasn't quite as good, but it was close," Gilder said with a smile.

The 1983 matches weren't well attended by fans or the media. But they were a sign of what was to come. Four years earlier, at Nicklaus's urging, European players had been added to those from Great Britain–Ireland to make the event more competitive.

After his team barely won in 1983, Nicklaus said, "We will not be the favorites when we go to the Belfry in two years. This [close] score was no fluke."

The Ryder Cup was on its way to gaining fan interest and status on a level with golf's major championships, and Bob Gilder had been a big part of the beginning.

I began writing about Gilder shortly after he graduated from Corvallis (Oregon) High School and took up golf seriously. He was raw and, with no scholarship offers, went to Arizona State University as a walk-on. Patience and hard work paid off, though, and he eventually earned a scholarship while joining such pros-to-be teammates as Tom Purtzer, Howard Twitty and Morris Hatalsky.

Before heading to ASU, he played in an amateur tournament in Salem, Oregon, and was matched against Bob Norquist, then the Oregon Golf Association's director of junior golf.

"He won the last hole to beat me one-up," Norquist said. "He shook my hand and told me what a honor it had been to play me. Just a fantastic guy, but I didn't think he would make it at Arizona State. Shows how much I know."

Bob Gilder, here hitting a pitch shot in a 1991 tournament, was a key figure for the United States team as it edged Europe in the 1983 Ryder Cup matches at Palm Beach Gardens, Florida. *Photo by Michael Lloyd/*Oregonian.

Gilder, an admitted golf grinder with a homemade swing, went on to win six times on the PGA Tour, including the Phoenix Open in his second tour tournament. He claimed his tenth Champions Tour title when he rallied from behind Mark Brooks to win the Principal Charity Classic in the spring of 2011.

Of his unorthodox swing, on which he finishes with his weight on his back foot, Gilder once said, "Some people learn how to score, and other people learn how to make a beautiful swing. I didn't care about a beautiful swing."

Doug Tewell, Gilder's friend and fellow pro, said, "When Bob is on, he is as good as anybody."

I interviewed Gilder often over the years as he continued to live in Corvallis and put up with travel inconveniences to play the tour. I watched with admiration as he took the unpopular stance and didn't abandon Ping Golf's Karsten Solheim at the time of Solheim's suit against the PGA Tour over square grooves. But the most fun I had working with him came at the 1983 Ryder Cup.

It began the day before the matches when Gilder's wife, Peggy, told me, "Bob is just so thrilled to be here."

When I talked to him that day, he admitted to being revved up about having dinner and a team meeting that night at Nicklaus's nearby home. At this meeting, he overheard Tom Watson talking to Nicklaus and saying, "I would like to be paired with Bob Gilder because he plays aggressively, just like I do."

"That made me feel so good," Gilder said. "I was on cloud nine."

Gilder, who earned his berth on the United States team with three tour victories in 1982, went two and two in his four matches. In a four-ball match on the second day, he and Watson were six under par in defeating Sam Torrance and Ian Woosnam five and four. They repeatedly fired at difficult pin settings and left themselves with a surplus of good birdie putts.

Gilder and Watson weren't so successful later that same day in foursomes, losing two and one to the hot-shooting Ballesteros and Paul Way. Gilder's other match, a foursomes pairing with Raymond Floyd on opening day, turned into a four-and-three loss to Canizares and Torrance as the Americans both played erratically.

When it was over, Gilder still looked like one of the tour's quiet men, but I sensed that he had picked up a large dose of confidence. Perhaps that confidence was a key to his later success, particularly on the Champions Tour.

"I'll never forget that [Ryder Cup] experience," he said. "It was awesome."

Chapter 8

THE "KING OF THE COAST"

Amateur Ralph Dichter had faced and survived many difficult challenges in golf, but nothing quite like the one he got from club pro Boots Porterfield in the 1966 Oregon Open at Waverley Country Club. Porterfield gave it to him, along with the biggest grin he could muster, on the ninth tee of the course in the Portland suburbs.

Porterfield and Dichter were paired together that day and were playing solid golf when they came to their final hole of the tournament's opening round—the 122-yard ninth. I was next to the nearby scoreboard with my back to the ninth green.

Suddenly, there was commotion behind me, and a spectator said, "Hey, Bob, who is that guy? He just made a hole in one." I looked back toward the tee and told him that it was Porterfield. Then I turned back to the scoreboard and talked to a tournament official about Porterfield's shot. Then there was more commotion, and again, I was asked to identify another player who had made a hole in one. I identified him as Dichter.

By that time, I was feeling extremely foolish. The National Hole-in-One Registry once estimated the odds of players making back-to-back aces at seventeen million to one, and I hadn't seen either one of them on this day despite being within a few yards of the hole. At least I had good material for a story.

The story got even better when I learned that Porterfield and Dichter had been exchanging friendly needles throughout the round. When Porterfield made his ace with an eight-iron, he turned to Dichter and issued the challenge: "Let's see you match that." Dichter used a nine-iron for his ace and then said to Porterfield, "Will that do?"

Porterfield finished with a sixty-eight and Dichter with a sixty-nine. They seemed to take delight in kidding me after they learned that I had been looking the other way on both of their historic shots.

Over the years, I had occasion to write many stories about Dichter, most of them for feats at his home Astoria Golf and Country Club. His golf play there became legendary. Included were a record ten titles in the Men's Grand Championship Division of the Oregon Coast Invitational, a match-play event for men and women with fields of up to four hundred players.

In addition, he finished as runner-up on eight other occasions. He also was a qualifying medalist six times, three times with five-under-par sixty-sevens. Later, he claimed three Junior-Seniors titles and one Super Seniors crown. Long ago, someone referred to him as "King of the Coast," and the nickname stuck.

To show Dichter's command of Astoria Golf and Country Club, his eclectic score (lowest total on each hole for his career) was a stunning thirty-three-under-par thirty-nine. Included were a hole in one and fourteen eagles. "I actually had four aces on the seventeenth hole, but I couldn't get one on any of the other par-threes," he said.

During a 2010 interview on the occasion of the tournament's one-hundredth anniversary, Dichter shared some memories with me that brought a twinkle to his eyes. Then eighty-five, he no longer was able to play in his favorite tournament because of health issues, but that hadn't changed his interest in it.

As background, the tournament began at nearby Gearhart Golf Links in 1910 and was called the Gearhart Summer Championship. It was contested mainly among members of Portland-area country clubs. There were stops and starts. There were no stagings in 1918, in 1927–31 or during the World War II years of 1942–45. There was also a move to Astoria Golf and Country Club for four years before a return to Gearhart after the war.

Finally, Gearhart course owner Bill Wilcox determined that the event had outgrown his facility and sold it to Astoria Golf and Country Club in 1951 for a token five dollars.

"Wilcox turned over the trophies that he had ready, and we used them," Dichter said. That's when the tournament, which had been renamed the Oregon Coast Invitational, began its steady growth in popularity.

Dichter claimed his first title in 1952 and won three times in a row in 1964–66. But before that, he had perhaps his most memorable final in 1949

Ralph Dichter (right) shakes hands with Bob Duden before their historic finals match in the 1949 Oregon Coast Invitational. Duden finally won in forty-two holes. *Courtesy of Astoria Golf and Country Club.*

at Gearhart. Matched against Bob Duden, later to become a renowned pro in the Pacific Northwest, Dichter lost in a historic forty-two-hole match.

"That was a marathon," Dichter said. "In the extra holes, we both made birdies on the third. Then he finally got me with a birdie on the sixth."

Dichter has special memories of two of his other title matches—against Jerry Cundari in 1964 and against Ed Vranizan in the Junior-Seniors in 1979.

He beat Cundari with a spectacular birdie on the thirty-seventh hole after Cundari's three-putt green at the thirty-sixth gave his opponent unexpected new life.

"I thought it was all over [at the thirty-sixth hole]," Dichter said. "I gave my glove to my caddie and told him what to do with my clubs. I was shocked when Jerry three-putted."

Of the extra hole, Cundari, a former University of Oregon golf star, recalled, "Ralph hit the most amazing three-wood shot from a sidehill lie to about two feet. I had a miserable drive home to Portland that day, but Ralph and I became special friends after that."

Dichter won the first six holes against Vranizan but, incredibly, still lost one-up. "I think I had a focus problem with the big lead, but Ed played very well," he said.

It was a typical reaction from Dichter, who had an impressive knack for being humble in victory and gracious in defeat. Kind of fitting, too, from someone carrying the nickname "King of the Coast."

Chapter 9
PEBBLE'S MONSTER MODE

Tom Shaw arrived at the Pebble Beach Golf Links for the 1972 U.S. Open with considerable confidence. His game was on an upswing, and he had positive memories from his two-shot victory over Arnold Palmer on the course in the 1971 Bing Crosby National Pro-Amateur, commonly called the Crosby Clambake in those days.

Little did the former University of Oregon golf standout know that, along with his fellow pros, he was about to be introduced to the famous course's monster mode.

After tying for the lead with a one-under-par seventy-one in the opening round, the easygoing Shaw said, "The course is playing awfully tough, but I think somebody can shoot four under par."

Pebble Beach, located on a craggy coastline above Carmel Bay in California's Monterey Peninsula, has frequently been referred to as a national treasure. Challenging and sporty, it provides scenic beauty that can take your breath away. The upscale public course's character hasn't changed much over the years, with coastal weather almost always a factor in how it plays for golfers of all levels. It became hugely popular despite escalating green fees.

Still, it wasn't until 1972, when Pebble Beach played host to its first U.S. Open, that it showed what a monster it could become when set up by the United States Golf Association for its showcase championship.

The monster mode came for the first time in the final round that year and repeated itself in the final round of the 1992 Open, both times when howling winds gusted to between thirty and forty miles per hour and left most of the game's finest players unable to execute normal shots.

I happened to be at both of those Opens, and the experience was riveting. The weird thing was that, in both cases, temperatures were mild and the weather was fine for spectators whose major concern was keeping hats from blowing off.

In 1972, Jack Nicklaus held the lead by one shot heading into the closing round. Then he shot a two-over-par seventy-four to finish at two-over 290. That was good enough to win by three strokes over Bruce Crampton and by four over Palmer, both of whom finished with seventy-sixes.

Nicklaus, who had four birdies, three bogeys and a double-bogey that day, said, "I played a good round of golf, an awfully good round." When Nicklaus gives acclaim to a seventy-four, it speaks volumes about the degree of difficulty he faced.

"I can't recall a day when we came so close to not being able to play the game of golf," he added. "There were times when skill almost was eliminated as a factor."

The wind, sometimes switching directions to add confusion, blew shots off line, made judging distances a guessing game and made playing approaches to the greens a nightmare.

The wind dried out the greens to crusty, linoleum-like hardness and, because of the daily triple cutting by USGA's order, the grass on them began to die midway through that final round. Holding an iron shot on them was not impossible but almost so.

The carnage was immense. Lee Trevino and Gary Player had 78s, Johnny Miller a 79, Lanny Wadkins an 81 and Hale Irwin and Tony Jacklin both had 83s. George Archer shot an 87 and claimed he did it despite taking just twenty-four putts. The scoring average for the final round was a whopping 78.8 with only two players shooting par or better.

Shaw, who had dropped from contention earlier, closed with a seventy-seven that ended up not looking too bad. "I played well, but I missed about four little putts of between three and four feet," he said.

Considering the conditions, it was amazing that Nicklaus could hit one of the greatest shots of his career that day. It came at the 218-yard seventeenth hole, the same hole on which Tom Watson sank his improbable chip shot on his way to victory in the 1982 Open.

Nicklaus used a one-iron for the shot into the wind, and the ball tracked directly at the pin. It cleared a protecting bunker, took one bounce, hit the flagstick and stopped within inches of the cup. The tap-in birdie clinched his thirteenth major championship. "I think, if the pin had been leaning the right way, the ball might have gone in," Nicklaus said.

I didn't anticipate that I would ever see such a tournament finish again. But I was wrong, because the circumstances were extremely similar in 1992. Scoring was better in the early rounds, but when the players showed up for the final eighteen, another mild day for spectators turned into a torture chamber for the golfers as the winds came roaring in off the Pacific Ocean.

Just as in 1972, scores soared, and the game became a survival test, which Tom Kite finally won with a 3-under-par 285. Just like Nicklaus in 1972, he was severely tested. And just like Nicklaus, he managed a miraculous shot along the way.

This was the Open in which Gil Morgan shot the lights out for two rounds, plus seven holes of the third round. He became the first player to reach double-digits under par in an Open. His birdie on the seventh hole of the third round even got him to twelve under and into a seven-shot lead.

Oregon entry Bob Gilder, discouraged by strong coastal winds in the final round of the 1992 U.S. Open, was stunned to learn that his seventy-four had moved him from twenty-eighth to sixth place. *Photo by Michael Lloyd/ Oregonian.*

Then Morgan went into a tailspin, going seven over par on the next five holes. With a seventy-seven, he still had the lead at four-under 212 heading into the final round. But a bunch of players were back in the hunt, including Kite, who had quietly moved into a three-way tie for second with a 70 and 213.

That set the stage for another attention-grabbing finish with soaring scores that embarrassed many players. Morgan struggled to an 81, but he hardly was alone. Seve Ballesteros and Ian Woosnam had 79s; Mark Calcavecchia, Peter Jacobsen and Paul Azinger, 80s; Craig Stadler and Raymond Floyd, 81s; Payne Stewart, an 83; Mark Brooks, an 84; and Scott Simpson, an 88. The average score for the day was 77.3.

There were bizarre moments in the late going. First, Colin Montgomerie managed to get in with a superb 70 for an even-par 288. Nicklaus, thinking no one could match that, congratulated Montgomerie (on the tournament telecast) for his "victory."

Then Jeff Sluman made an eighteenth-hole birdie for a 71 and took the lead at 287.

All the while, Kite kept grinding away. He hit his miraculous shot at the testy 107-yard seventh after he pulled his tee shot, with a crosswind's help, sixty feet left of the pin in deep rough. But with a bogey or worse looming, he pitched the ball into the hole for a most improbable birdie, giving him the lead.

He built his edge to as much as four and, despite bogeys at the sixteenth and seventeenth holes, won with a closing seventy-two.

"This was not close to my best tournament tee to green," Kite said. "But, for hanging in there, it probably was my best. It was gut-check time out there."

I had an amusing experience when Oregon player Bob Gilder finished with a seventy-four. He was upset about not doing better. "Your round wasn't that bad," I told him. He rolled his eyes in my direction before walking away with his head down.

Later, I crossed paths with Gilder after he learned that his seventy-four had lifted him from a tie for twenty-eighth place to a tie for sixth. He smiled and said, "I guess I did a little better than I thought."

When Pebble Beach is set up for a U.S. Open and the wind goes crazy, it can be that confusing.

Chapter 10

JOHNSON'S LABOR OF LOVE

We were on the drive from Portland to Central Oregon for a pro-amateur at Prineville Country Club, and Dale Johnson was filling me in on the course, which I hadn't played.

"The one thing you have to be careful about is the rattlesnakes," he said. "They're in the surrounding area. They sometimes come down off the hill to the edge of the fairways to sun themselves."

Johnson knew about my dread of snakes, even the garden variety, and I should have been smart enough to figure out that I was being set up. I wasn't.

Anyway, we began our practice round, and I kept the ball in play nicely until I reached the third hole, where my drive sailed to the right into a sandy area with large rocks and clumps of sagebrush. I was on snake alert. I approached my ball cautiously, took a three-iron from my bag and prepared to hit.

Just as I took my club back, there was this rattlesnake-like sound from behind me. I dropped my club and ran toward the fairway. Then I saw Johnson, bent over in laughter, and realized that he had snuck up behind me and done his best rattlesnake imitation.

"I bet you've never jumped that high in your life," he said.

It's just one of the stories I remember about Johnson, a legend in Pacific Northwest golf circles for his long and creative service to the game.

Johnson retired at the end of 1989, after serving as executive secretary of the Pacific Northwest PGA and the Oregon Golf Association for twenty-five years. A longtime Portland resident, he was eighty when he died in 2005.

But his is a true case of gone but not forgotten. He meant that much to the game he loved. His was a heartwarming success story.

Johnson admitted that he became a golf official almost by accident. It began in 1960 after the death of George Bertz, a longtime sports editor of the *Oregon Journal* who had been helping the OGA with some of its activities. Johnson, a former golf writer for the *Oregonian*, took his place—"because I knew I wanted to work in golf in some capacity." Initially, he was paid fifty dollars a month for his service.

His first office was in the basement of his home. It snowballed from there.

"When I started as executive secretary [of the two groups] in 1964, there were only two other PGA sections that had secretaries—Southern California and Georgia," he said. "By 1980, all but two sections had full-time secretaries."

By the time of his death, Johnson had the satisfaction of knowing that the OGA had blossomed into one of the top organizations of its type in the country. It even had its own OGA Golf Course with executive offices next to the clubhouse in Woodburn. It was some kind of step-up from those days when Johnson worked alone in his basement.

Dale was one of my closest friends, and he was a mentor to me in my early days covering golf for the *Oregonian*. He was the same friend and mentor for Bill Mulflur, executive sports editor of the *Oregon Journal* before it was merged with the *Oregonian* in 1982.

"Dale wasn't just a jock, either," Mulflur said. "Sure, he liked sports, but he was a well-rounded person with a lot of other interests."

Perhaps his strongest forte in golf was as a rules official. He was a master at knowing the rulebook from cover to cover.

"There is a difference between knowing the rules and knowing how to apply them correctly," said Jim Gibbons, who learned from Johnson and became a rules expert himself while serving as executive director of the OGA. "That's where Dale really excelled."

On the lighter side, his storytelling skills undoubtedly also will play a major role in keeping memories of him alive.

Take this one about his play as a sophomore for his high school golf team in Nampa, Idaho.

"It was the 1941 state tournament, and we had a good team," he said. "I was playing late [in the final round], and when I came to the last hole, it was cut and dried. If I could make a par on the hole, a par-five, we would win the championship. If I made a six, we would tie. So I hit my drive out of bounds and made a seven. We had come to the tournament in a van.

The other guys on the team wouldn't let me ride home with them. I had to catch a bus."

Then there was the one about all-time great Walter Hagen.

"When I heard people talk about what a playboy Walter was, how he would come to the course in his tuxedo and with a hangover, it amused me," Johnson said. "I knew differently. I once was a correspondent for *Golf World* and was well acquainted with Bob Harlow, the magazine's founder.

"Harlow also was Hagen's manager, and he was one of the all-time promoters. He knew exactly how to get the most out of golf for Hagen, by giving him a playboy image. Hell, in his prime, Hagen would get ten hours of sleep before his tournament rounds. Then Harlow would get him up, dress him in shirt and tails, poor some booze over his head and send him to the golf course. I know it happened that way. I saw it."

In his officiating capacity, Johnson followed a strict code. "When I was called out onto the course, I did my best to not know which player was involved," he said. "In my position, I had to rule only on the situation. The person involved was irrelevant."

Of course, not knowing was often difficult. That was the case one year at the Sunriver Oregon Open when Don Bies pulled his drive on one hole of the resort's Woodlands Course into what he thought was a molehill. Playing companion Rick Acton disagreed and called for Johnson to make a ruling. After a careful look, Johnson ruled that the ball was indeed in a molehill and that Bies was entitled to relief.

"I knew you would do that," Acton said.

"If you thought that, why did you ask me to come out here?" Johnson said.

At times, he had to be creative with his interpretations. One such occasion was an Oregon PGA Pro-Amateur when an amateur pulled his drive, and the ball embedded in a nearby ball washer. Johnson was called for a ruling. After a few moments of contemplation, he said, "Casual water, free drop."

There were times when making the correct ruling was a thankless task. One time, in a Pacific Northwest Golf Association Women's Championship in British Columbia, Johnson was ripped by the media after he informed a match's referee about the proper ruling on a free drop. The ruling gave an American a good break and led to an eventual victory over a Canadian. A newspaper the next day had a headline about the Canadian player being robbed.

"I was glad to get out of town," Johnson said. "A guy shouldn't have to make rulings in a foreign country."

Dale had some embarrassing moments, too. Probably the most embarrassing came the day before a pro-amateur in Hood River, when he played a practice round with Oregon club pro Harvey Hixson.

"After we had played a few holes, Hixson pointed at me," Johnson said. "He turned to a friend who was in the foursome and said, 'If you want to know anything about the rules, just ask this guy. He's an expert.'

"The friend grinned and replied to Harvey, 'If he knows so much about the rules, how come he just hit my ball?' I looked down, and sure enough, I had hit his ball. I felt ridiculous."

Dale didn't mind laughing at himself. It was just another of his special qualities.

Chapter II

IT WAS A CHALLENGE

It's not likely that Peter Jacobsen will forget the day. He and Ed Ellis were at Portland Golf Club on the morning after the inaugural Fred Meyer Challenge in 1986. Everything had gone well for Jacobsen, the tournament's host, and Ellis, the chief of operations, except for one major detail.

"We had forgotten to arrange for a [post-tournament] garbage pickup," Jacobsen said. "So how was that for a comedown? Curtis Strange and I had tied for the title [with Greg Norman and Gary Player] the day before, but there I was the next day picking up cigarette butts."

That's the way it began as Jacobsen and tournament co-founder Mike Stoll saw their dream come true, a special golfing event bringing some of the game's biggest names to Portland. They didn't want it to be "just an exhibition," either, but a competition that would be significant enough to get the players' juices flowing. They anticipated correctly that two-player teams in a best-ball format would provide that and be popular with the fans.

I wondered about their optimism at the time, but the Challenge simply took off, becoming the premier non–PGA Tour event in the country and the harbinger of golf's so-called silly season. It ran for seventeen stagings at three venues in the Portland area—Oregon Golf Club and the Reserve Vineyards and Golf Club in addition to Portland Golf Club.

"This is the best unofficial golf tournament in existence," said Arnold Palmer after the fourth staging. "It gets more attention than a lot of tour events."

Peter Jacobsen bumps fists with Arnold Palmer, his traditional partner, in the 2011 Umpqua Bank Challenge at Portland Golf Club. Palmer also played in all seventeen of the Fred Meyer Challenges from 1986 to 2002. *Photo by Jon Ferry.*

Palmer proved it wasn't idle chatter by participating in every Challenge, most of them as Jacobsen's partner. It was a huge endorsement boost for a tournament in a small-market area.

When Fred Meyer, a variety store chain, went under new ownership and withdrew as title sponsor after the 2002 tournament, Jacobsen's management company went in a different direction. It became involved in presentation of the Champion Tour's Jeld-Wen Tradition at the Reserve and then the Sunriver Resort in Central Oregon from 2003 through 2010. It never caught on with the fans the way the Challenge had.

"We never really wanted the Challenge to end; it just worked out that way," Jacobsen said.

So, when the Tradition moved on after its 2010 staging, he was quick to revive a scaled-down version of the Challenge in 2011 at Portland Golf Club with Umpqua Bank as the title sponsor. Many fans seemed to welcome it back like a long lost friend.

Over the years, the Challenge's format didn't change much. In addition to the competition, there were two highly popular clinics, a pro-amateur and a gala dinner party for pro-am participants and corporate sponsors with the players in attendance.

There were rocky times along the way. Stoll departed after the 1988 staging following contract disagreements with the title sponsor. Suddenly, it was Jacobsen's show, and he responded smoothly with a new management company, now called Peter Jacobsen Sports. Ellis was tournament director at first in the new regime, eventually becoming the company's president until 2005.

The Challenge's success showed in its contributions to ten children's charities—more than $10 million over its initial seventeen-tournament run.

It puzzled me for a long time why the Challenge would remain so popular with little change in what it offered from year to year. I finally came to the conclusion that it was the offbeat nature of the event, its sideshows, the pro-am celebrities and the fans' opportunity to interact with the players that won the day. Jacobsen often described the Challenge as "not your usual golf tournament," and that's just what it stayed over the years.

There were dozens of highlights on the course, starting with Norman's thirty-foot putt for a birdie at the final hole in 1986 that forced Jacobsen to make a seven-footer for a par and a co-championship. "I don't know that I've ever been more nervous on a putt," Jacobsen said. "All my friends were right there watching."

Norman and Brad Faxon teamed up to win three titles in a row, a startling feat considering the caliber of players they were up against. After the third victory in 1997, Norman said, "It's a bunch of crap that we are just here having fun. We play to win whether or not it is a tour tournament, and Brad and I had a lot of good players chasing us today."

Payne Stewart holed an improbable fifty-foot eagle putt at Portland Golf Club's fifteenth hole in 1987, leading him and Isao Aoki to a two-shot win. The late Stewart embodied much of what the Challenge was about, commiserating with spectators, playing his harmonica as part of "Jake Trout and the Flounders" with Jacobsen and Mark Lye and auctioning off the pants he was wearing at one of the early tournament parties.

Then there was a playoff in 1991 at Portland Golf Club that ended abruptly at the par-three seventeenth hole, the second of the playoff. Ben Crenshaw rolled in a curling thirty-five-footer for a birdie that gave him and Paul Azinger the victory over the teams of Raymond Floyd–Fred Couples and Bob Gilder–Mark Calcavecchia. "The best way to describe Ben's putting is to say that he feeds the ball into the hole," Azinger said.

Most members of the 1991 U.S. Ryder Cup team, along with captain Dave Stockton, were in the field that year.

Peter Jacobsen, his shirt filled with golf balls, does his imitation of Craig Stadler at one of the clinics that became so popular at the Fred Meyer Challenge and now the Umpqua Bank Challenge. *Photo by Jon Ferry.*

On the flip side, there was Couples's stunning four-putt from eight feet in 1992 at Oregon Golf Club's par-five thirteenth hole. It turned a likely eagle into a bogey for him and partner Davis Love III in the final round and probably cost them the title. Billy Andrade, playing in the same foursome, made his eagle putt and charged to victory with partner Tom Kite.

I approached Couples cautiously after the round, figuring he might be in no mood to talk. But he was his usual honest self. "I just started flinching," said the man who had won the Masters earlier in the year.

Teams threatened to break sixty several times in the Challenge, and it finally happened in 2001 at the Reserve when Tom Lehman and Sergio Garcia shot fifty-nine. Unbelievably, thirty minutes later, Fuzzy Zoeller and Jean Van de Velde came in with a fifty-seven.

Then there was the year that Stewart and Stadler were partners, and Stewart talked Stadler into wearing matching knickers. Stadler in knickers was a stunning sight that delighted spectators.

Probably just as significant to the Challenge's popularity as the tournament itself were the clinics, with Jacobsen as master of ceremonies. It's amazing how his imitations of players such as Palmer, Kite, Floyd, Stadler, Lee Trevino and Johnny Miller never seemed to get old.

At times, the clinics were like a vaudeville act. One year at Oregon Golf Club, I was enthralled right along with everybody else when Palmer and Jack Nicklaus took over, needling each other, showing off trick shots and challenging each other to match shots. One-liners flew, and when Jacobsen tried to be a part of it, Nicklaus waved him away and said, "This is a two-man act."

One of my favorite clinic happenings also came in 1992 when Jacobsen was having Larry Mize demonstrate shots. "OK, Larry, let's see you reenact that chip shot that won you the [1987] Masters playoff with Greg Norman," Jacobsen said.

Mize, looking sheepish, took his pitching wedge and walked down the incline in front of Oregon Golf Club's eighteenth green. When he got about 140 feet from the pin—the distance of his famed shot at Augusta National's eleventh hole—he dropped a ball, studied the terrain and, amazingly, sank the shot. Then, after a collective gasp from approximately five thousand spectators, Mize did his best to mimic his 1987 victory celebration. Norman, also an entry that year, offered a weak smile from his seat beside the green.

At the 1994 clinic, Jacobsen had Phil Mickelson and Crenshaw show off their putting strokes. Suddenly, he asked them to exchange putters. That meant that lefty Mickelson would putt right-handed, and righty Crenshaw would go from the left side. Mickelson sank a twenty-footer on his first try. Crenshaw narrowly missed twice before connecting on his third effort.

Mickelson always was one of the most popular players at the clinics, with his trick shots and short-game wizardry. At the Reserve one year, he was demonstrating chip and sand shots from about eighty feet. It didn't take him long to roll a chip into the cup. Then he said, "OK, let's spin one." What followed was like magic, as he pitched a ball that landed about two feet behind the hole and crawled back in. Beside the green, his fellow pros stood and bowed.

Obviously, there were few set scripts at the clinics, and that certainly was true in 1993 before the pro-amateur at Oregon Golf Club. John Daly was hitting towering drives that were drawing oohs and aahs from the gallery. Then, unexpectedly, he turned around and launched a drive over the heads of spectators who were sitting on a hillside behind the eighteenth green.

Jacobsen was left speechless, but Palmer wasn't the next day after arriving for the tournament. "That was the most ridiculous thing I've heard of in a long time," he said. "He could have killed someone." The PGA Tour issued a fine to Daly, believed to have been $30,000, for his indiscretion.

John Daly takes the kind of explosive swing that he used to nail a controversial drive over the heads of spectators at the 1993 Fred Meyer Challenge at Oregon Golf Club. *Photo by Michael Lloyd/Oregonian.*

The Challenge always offered outstanding celebrities—Jack Lemmon, Michael Jordan, Clint Eastwood, Jerry West, Neil Armstrong, Chad Everett, Randy Quaid, Susan Anton, Glenn Frey and Huey Lewis among them. The gem of them all, though, was Bob Hope in 1989.

"I'll never forget his entrance," Jacobsen said. Then eighty-six, Hope was a late arrival and drove a golf cart up the eighteenth fairway at Portland Golf Club, bringing the in-progress clinic to a hand-clapping standstill. He played just eight holes of the pro-am that day, but fans flocked to him.

Later, I had a chance to interview Hope, my first and only time. It was a delightful experience, and I found him to be just like in his slapstick performances on the stage. The one-liners just seemed to come so naturally.

Such as: "I'm playing so lousy that Titleist offered me fifty dollars not to use its ball."

Such as: "[Former] President Gerald Ford was the first man in history to make golf a contact sport."

Such as: "I have to talk to my body in the morning and see just what it is willing to do."

In a way, Hope's popular theme song, "Thanks for the Memories," might have been a good adoption for the Fred Meyer Challenge.

Chapter 12

ONE COLORFUL BUNNY

Jack Nicklaus was off to a blazing start in 1962, his rookie year on the PGA Tour. He already had won the U.S. Open and the Seattle World's Fair Open when he arrived in Portland for the Portland Open at Columbia Edgewater Country Club. There, he ran into the crosshairs of Gene "Bunny" Mason, the Columbia Edgewater head pro.

Understand, Mason was much more than a club pro in those days. He also was a national vice-president of the PGA of America, which, at the time, had the PGA Tour as one of its wings. And he thought that Nicklaus needed to be disciplined for what he felt was unnecessarily slow play.

Early in the week, Mason said he approached a tour operations manager. "I told him I would have his job if he didn't do something about [the speed of Nicklaus's play]," he said. "I thought the example he was setting was bad for the game."

Whether or not Mason's threat was a deciding factor is unclear, but Nicklaus was penalized two strokes in the second round by rules official Joe Black. He was given the word before signing his scorecard after shooting a sixty-seven while playing with Billy Casper and Bruce Crampton. Casper, a fast player, and Crampton, a slow one, were not penalized.

So, Nicklaus's sixty-seven became a sixty-nine. He was furious at first and declined to be interviewed for more than thirty minutes. Then, he calmly came to the media room and firmly expressed his disapproval of the "unfair ruling."

I had followed the group that day and thought that Nicklaus had at least some justification for being upset. The threesome finished in a reasonable time but had fallen two holes behind the group in front of it. Mostly, it seemed to me, that was because of delays brought about by an overflow of spectators that made gallery ropes inadequate.

Nicklaus didn't let the penalty bother his play in the final two rounds. He shot sixty-seven and sixty-nine and, with a score of nineteen-under-par 269, won by one stroke over George Bayer.

Before departing after the awards ceremony, Mason said Nicklaus came to the pro shop and gave him a parting shot: "Go to hell; I won anyway."

Mason laughed as he told the story. "I still think that one of the best moves I made as a PGA vice-president was getting Nicklaus penalized," he said.

Twenty-five years later, while in Portland for the Fred Meyer Challenge, Nicklaus said, "I probably deserved the penalty, but if I did, so did Bruce and Billy. That's why I was so hot when I got the ruling."

Later, in his book *Jack Nicklaus: My Story with Ken Bowden* (Simon and Schuster, 1997), he wrote, "When I became engrossed in competing, I tended to immerse myself in a cocoon of concentration that simply precluded awareness of such trivialities as time."

Mason, who was eighty-one when he died in 2010, did much more productive things while serving as a PGA officer. The most significant was his founding of the PGA Education Program and Business Schools, which made it possible for club pros to attain the status of other professionally trained people. He was selected for the PGA's Horton Smith Trophy in 1966 for his contributions.

He also was active as a member and officer of the PGA's Pacific Northwest Section, earning Golf Professional of the Year and Teacher of the Year awards in addition to being named to the organization's Hall of Fame. He had his moments as a player, too, winning the 1956 Oregon Open at the Eastmoreland municipal course in Portland and qualifying for multiple U.S. Opens and PGA Championships.

In his later years, Mason designed more than a dozen golf courses in the Northwest, and after a management stint at the Black Butte Ranch Resort in Central Oregon, he returned to teaching golf at Columbia Edgewater. Among his pupils was 1972 U.S. Women's Amateur champion Mary Budke.

"By the time Mary came to me, all she needed was a little work on refinements," he said.

At the same time, Mason was witty, fun loving, a superb storyteller and always looking to needle a friend. On the golf course, his motto seemed to be "play fast, have fun and don't take yourself too seriously."

I first got to know Mason after he became the pro at Salem Golf Club in the early 1950s. Before that, I had watched him play some football and basketball games at Salem High School (later renamed North Salem) and in a brief career as a player for the Salem Trailblazers in the Northwest Professional Basketball League.

Mason, who had his unusual nickname from childhood, also played briefly on the team that toured and provided opposition for the Harlem Globetrotters. "The Trotters properly intimidated and humiliated me in my first game," he said. "They made me into an excellent straight man."

Gene "Bunny" Mason shows a big smile as he is inducted into the Pacific Northwest PGA Hall of Fame in 1980. *Courtesy of Pacific Northwest PGA.*

The lanky Mason was seldom a straight man after that. He was an expert at dishing out humor and forcing the straight-man role onto others. He also seemed to have more than his share of strange experiences in golf.

One year, while playing in the Crosby Clambake (before it became the AT&T Pebble Beach Pro-Amateur), Mason was even-par for a round at Cypress Point through sixteen holes before making a nine on the par-four seventeenth. Asked what happened, he borrowed from a Walter Hagen line and replied, "I missed an eight-footer for my eight." Actually, he took four shots to escape from an ice plant.

At a pro-amateur at Michelbook Country Club in McMinnville, Oregon, he left a twenty-foot birdie putt hanging on the lip of the cup and tossed his hat into the air. It came down on top of the ball, moving it slightly, necessitating a penalty. The incident became known among his fellow pros as the "Mason Hat Trick."

He once had eight penalty strokes in nine holes in the old Pendleton (Oregon) Open. His problems included a ball hitting a sprinkler head and bouncing out of bounds, another ball hitting a rock in the fairway and bouncing out of bounds and a ball hitting a tree before rebounding into his caddie, bringing an automatic two-stroke penalty. "On top of that, after hitting my caddie, the ball ended up in the divot hole that I had just made," he said.

My favorite Mason story, though, involved his confrontation with tour pro Phil Rodgers at the 1963 Portland Open at Columbia Edgewater. As the host pro, he had a strict rule that no player or caddie could go into the bag storage room. An assistant pro was at the door at all times during the tournament to either get a player's clubs or to put them away.

"Al Mundle [his top assistant] was on the door this day when Rodgers came up and said that his caddie was going in to get his clubs," Mason said. "Al said no, that he would get the clubs, and Rodgers pushed him. I happened to be close by and came over and said I would get the clubs. Rodgers's caddie followed me. I stopped and waved him back. Quite frankly, I was hot. I had had a couple of other problems with Rodgers in the past, and I didn't like him."

Anyway, when Mason returned through the doorway with Rodgers's clubs, he slung them across the blacktop, some of them slithering out of the bag and into a rose bush. "I told him to keep his clubs in his car for the rest of the tournament," Mason said.

Mundle recalled that "it was a pretty wild scene."

Rodgers, one of the tour's top players at the time, shot 279 and tied for eighteenth place that week.

The story had a sequel, too—two years later, when Mason qualified for the U.S. Open at Bellerive Country Club in St. Louis. He finished a practice round late and decided to have dinner in the clubhouse.

"There was hardly anyone in the dining room, but Rodgers was there, sitting by himself," Mason said. "He saw me and shouted, 'Hey, Bunny, why don't you join me for dinner?' I did, and we had a great, sociable evening. That was Phil—a strange fellow."

Interesting words to come from a character who wasn't exactly ordinary himself.

Chapter 13

MASTERS MOMENTS

It is often said that the Masters golf tournament doesn't really begin until the back nine of the final round, especially the last six holes. But, sometimes, key developments can come earlier, and luck can play a significant role. I saw just such situations while covering the 1992 and 1995 Masters.

Fred Couples, the pre-tournament favorite in 1992, pulled off a Houdini-like act at Augusta National Golf Club's treacherous twelfth hole in the final round. He saved a most unlikely par from a steep bank in front of the green and eventually scored a two-shot victory over Raymond Floyd.

"I thought, if I got by twelve OK, I was going to win," Couples said. He got by it—barely.

Brian Henninger, a journeyman player from Oregon in his first Masters in 1995, had stunned the field by sharing the third-round lead with former champion Ben Crenshaw. He was still tied with the Texan after both made pars on the final round's first hole. Then, at the par-five second, both players hit layup shots after mediocre drives, and their balls ended up within a couple feet of each other, about sixty-five yards short of the elongated green.

Henninger went first, and his sand-wedge approach missed by inches of carrying a bunker, which blocked the line to a tight pin setting. Then Crenshaw hit an almost identical shot that cleared the same bunker by no more than a foot and rolled to within five feet of the hole.

Crenshaw made his birdie putt, while Henninger failed to get up and down from the bunker and fell two shots behind with a bogey. Crenshaw went on to shoot a 68 for a fourteen-under-par finish at 274 and a one-shot win over Davis Love III. Henninger struggled to a 76 and a tie for tenth with Couples at 282.

"The shot into the bunker was just a hair short or the ball ends up three feet from the cup," a frustrated Henninger said.

Two shots, one averting disaster and the other breaking a magical spell of success, became so important in setting up what followed. They became a part of Masters lore.

Couples, seeking to win his first major championship, had been on an extended hot streak when he arrived in Augusta in 1992. He had won four times and had nineteen top-ten finishes in the preceding ten months.

"If I had to name seven or eight possible winners, Fred would be my number one choice," Jack Nicklaus said early in the week.

Couples was strong from the outset. Lanny Wadkins and Jeff Sluman led after the first round with 7-under-par 65s, while Couples was solid with a 69. He then shot a 67 for 136 and was one back of Ian Woosnam and Craig Parry.

It got confusing after that, with thunderstorms that delayed play in the third round and forced several players, including Couples, to finish their third rounds on Sunday before moving on to their final eighteens. Couples

Hitting big drives in front of large galleries never seemed to be a problem for Fred Couples, who used his power and accuracy to win the 1992 Masters. *Photo by Michael Lloyd/* Oregonian.

Fred Couples uses body English on this fairway wood shot in the Fred Meyer Challenge. *Photo by Michael Lloyd/*Oregonian.

completed his round in 69 and, at eleven-under 205, was one stroke behind Parry.

Then Couples began taking charge as Parry faded. By the time he stepped to the twelfth tee, he was three shots in front.

The 155-yard twelfth at Augusta is one of the scariest par-three holes in golf. The green is narrow from front to back, and Rae's Creek meanders in front of it with steep banking from the putting surface down to the water. Traditionally, the final-round pin setting is to the right, making the tee shot's carry longer and bringing the water more into play for anyone foolish enough to aim in that direction.

Couples had no intention of aiming at the pin with his eight-iron, but that's where the ball headed. From a media tower beside the twelfth tee, I could see that the shot was not going to be long enough. The ball landed on the bank and began its inevitable roll toward a watery grave. But spectators' groans turned to cheers when, amazingly, it hung up on a tuft of grass and stopped.

A look of agony on Couples's face was suddenly replaced by the look of someone who had gotten away with something. On his way to the green, he jogged more than walked. He was a man in a hurry. Wedge in hand, he was painstakingly careful not to ground his club for fear of dislodging the ball. Then, from an awkward stance, he chipped to within a foot to turn a potential double-bogey into a par.

"I was afraid the ball still might trickle down the bank while I was on my way to the green," said Couples, who finished his victory march with five pars and a birdie at the fourteenth.

Of his tee shot at the twelfth, he grinned and said, "My body tends to swing toward the flag no matter what I'm thinking. That was the luckiest break I've ever gotten in golf."

Henninger said he got goose bumps, as he anticipated, while driving down Magnolia Lane for the first time in 1995. The former University of

Southern California golfer, thirty-one at the time, admitted that he was in awe of the premises.

Too much in awe, perhaps, because he slipped four over par on the first five holes of his opening round. He looked like a player seeking a place to hide, not a green jacket. Somehow, though, he pulled himself together and made six birdies the rest of the way for a two-under-par seventy. He was just four shots out of the first-round lead.

Playing with Nick Faldo, Henninger made six more birdies in the second round for a sixty-eight and 138, three strokes behind leader Jay Haas and in a tie for seventh.

Amazingly, he kept right on making birdies in the third round—another six of them. The most exciting came at the sixteenth, a par-three with diabolical sloping in its green. With a pin setting to the right-front of the putting surface, Henninger saw his

Brian Henninger, who contended into the final round of the 1995 Masters, later became a popular figure at clinics, such as this one at the Children's Course in Gladstone, a Portland suburb. *Photo by Eric Yaillen/OGA.*

ball land in the middle of the green and then run slowly downhill to the left fringe, fifty feet from the cup. But playing "about twelve feet of break," he sank the putt, and the huge gallery roared. It was an incredulous moment.

"What has happened to him?" Henninger's mother, Carolyn, screamed from her vantage point near the green.

So for three rounds, Henninger had made eighteen birdies, more than anyone else in the field, and with a 68 for a 10-under 206, he was tied for the lead with Crenshaw.

"This has been a thrill for me and my family," Henninger said. "I just want the experience to go on and on."

It didn't. When he came to that second hole of the final round, it was as if all the magic suddenly went away. He had some decent chances but didn't make a single birdie that day.

Anyway, I was left to ponder the role luck had played and what might have been in both cases. Of course, there was no way of knowing.

Chapter 14

NANCY'S LAST STAND

The birdie putt crawled into the hole as if drawn by a magnet, and there was a cheer that escalated into a roar. Sheer joy showed in Nancy Lopez's smile. Then came a loud chant—"Nancy...Nancy...Nancy."

Lopez was back in the hunt in a U.S. Women's Open, and her loyal supporters were building up a head of steam.

It was the second round of the 1997 Open on Pumpkin Ridge Golf Club's Witch Hollow course, west of Portland. Lopez had just finished with her third consecutive birdie for a 4-under-par 68 and 137. She was tied for second, one shot behind surprising leader Alison Nicholas, who had a 66.

Crowds that had been good suddenly became record setting, and Lopez was the main attraction. Her popularity in the Portland area was off the charts. It had begun building way back in 1974 when she played in the U.S. Girls Junior Amateur at Columbia Edgewater Country Club.

I first saw her perform in that 1974 tournament, and it took her just two shots of a practice round to convince me that she was something special. She was seventeen and previously had won the tournament when she was fifteen. Playing the course's inside nine, she hit a long drive down the right side on the par-five first hole, set at about 455 yards that day. Then she nailed a four-iron second shot onto the green. Two-putt birdie. "This gal is going to be something else," I said to a nearby spectator.

Lopez breezed to victory that week, beating Lauren Howe seven and five in the final. A year later, still as an amateur, she qualified for the U.S. Women's Open and tied for second behind Sandra Palmer. No one, at the time, would

Nancy Lopez, who came so close to winning a coveted U.S. Women's Open title at Pumpkin Ridge in 1997, shows off her driving form during a guest appearance at the Albertsons Boise Open, a Nationwide Tour event. *Courtesy of Jeff Sanders Promotions.*

have thought for a second that she would finish second or tied for second four times in the Open but not be able to claim the title.

Now it was her last best chance, but that's getting ahead of the story.

Lopez became a fixture at Portland LPGA stops, collecting four victories. She and JoAnn Washam won the Portland Ping Team Championship at twenty-one-under par in 1979 at Portland Golf Club. She then won individual Portland titles in 1985 at Riverside Golf and Country Club and in 1987 and 1992 at Columbia Edgewater.

Seemingly thriving on drama, she made clutch shots and putts look routine, and fans flocked to her. Showing charm plus, she reacted openly to the fans—smiling, laughing, signing autographs. It was as if she had taken a preparatory course in golfer conduct from Arnold Palmer.

Typical was her performance in 1987, when she was four shots behind with nine holes to play at Columbia Edgewater. But she rallied and came to the final hole, a testing par-four, with a one-stroke lead and with the usual large crowd urging her on.

It was almost as if she had planned to give spectators a thrill when she left her second shot in shaggy rough to the right of the green. She needed a par to avoid a playoff with three other players. One of the others, Jan Stephenson, watched from behind the eighteenth green.

Lopez swung firmly through the rough and chipped the ball within four feet of the cup. Stephenson, who had missed a par putt from near the same spot, shook her head in dismay.

"Nancy never missed one of those in her life," she said. "That is her bread and butter. Anyone else, and I would have felt that I had a chance."

Stephenson then wheeled and headed for the locker room. She disappeared through the door just as Lopez sank the uphill putt with a slight left break to clinch the title.

After her Portland win in 1992, Lopez still had her charm, but she began a slow fade as an LPGA presence. Coming to Pumpkin Ridge, she had won just once in the previous four years. Only the most die-hard among her supporters could think that she had a legitimate chance to win the Open at age forty.

Then one of golf's most intriguing stories unfolded after Annika Sorenstam, the two-time defending champion, couldn't recover from a first-round seventy-seven and missed the cut.

The suspense increased in the third round over the 6,365-yard course, but Nicholas, a gritty competitor who had most of her success on the European Women's Tour, showed no signs of fading. Her 67 for 203 gave her a three-shot lead over Lopez, who had a 69.

In addition to her golf play, Nancy Lopez always was a popular participant at clinics such as this one at the Albertsons Boise Open. *Courtesy of Jeff Sanders Promotions.*

"I'm absolutely delighted," said Nicholas, who then told a story about being discouraged and on the verge of quitting professional golf in 1990—until Lopez talked her into not giving up. "She told me I should stick with it, and I did."

Lopez admitted to being "pumped up" by her contending position and by the undying devotion of her Portland-area fans. "I don't feel as if I have to win the Open, but it is the one I want," she said.

I figured, going into the final round, that it was going to be great theater, no matter the outcome. I thought of the great Sam Snead and how he never was able to win the men's U.S. Open. I wondered if Lopez, who had forty-eight career wins, was destined for similar frustration.

Being paired with Nicholas was just what Lopez wanted, and she figured her best chance for victory was to get a quick start. She did get a quick start, a spectacular one, with three birdies on the first four holes. Amazingly, though, she still was three strokes behind.

The drama was unbelievable at the par-five fourth hole after the two competitors found their balls only a couple feet apart after second shots. It was fifty-six yards to the cup for both of them, and Lopez lofted a wedge over a mound to within two feet. The crowd erupted in an arm-waving frenzy, anticipating a Lopez birdie, but the noise level dropped, then escalated again, when Nicholas sank her wedge shot for an eagle.

Lopez made her birdie but later admitted that it "felt like a bogey after Alison made that eagle."

Nicholas got her lead to four when Lopez made a bogey at the ninth, but Lopez kept battling back. She made a birdie at the thirteenth, and then Nicholas hit her approach shot over the green and into a hazard at the 393-yard fourteenth. The resulting double-bogey cut her lead to one.

This was turning into a finish as exciting as any in golf—men's or women's—and the gallery was into the whole thing. While almost exclusively rooting for Lopez, it showed respect for Nicholas. With the tension mounting, Lopez went bogey-birdie-bogey and Nicholas par-par-bogey on the next three holes. So, the two went to the par-five eighteenth with Nicholas still leading by one.

Finally, Lopez faced a downhill birdie putt from fifteen feet at the eighteenth, while Nicholas was left with a par putt of barely more than a foot. There were more than thirty thousand people at Pumpkin Ridge that day, but the silence was eerie as Lopez lined up her putt.

She struck it firmly but didn't play for quite enough break. The ball slipped three feet past. Tears welled up in Lopez's eyes, but she ignored them and made the comeback three-footer. Then Nicholas tapped in her putt for the victory.

"I got tears in my eyes, and I had a hard time seeing on the second putt," Lopez said. "I knew that one didn't matter, but I wanted to make it."

Nicholas, after a closing 71, finished at a 10-under-par 274, an Open record at the time for low score in relation to par. Lopez, who had a final-round 69, set a record, too. She became the first woman in Open history to post four scores in the sixties. That someone could do that and not win was unprecedented.

Lopez was still emotional through her post-tournament media session, frequently wiping away tears.

"Really, I'm happy with the way I played," she said. "Alison just went out and won the Open today."

Eight months later, I had a chance to interview Lopez at the Kraft Nabisco Championship. We talked about her experience at Pumpkin Ridge.

"At least I can talk about it now without tearing up," she said. "For a long time, I couldn't. I cried every time."

Chapter 15

THE PUMPKIN RIDGE DREAM

B ob Cupp tried to explain just what he was visualizing, but it was difficult for me to understand. He could visualize a world-class golf course. All I could see on that day early in 1990 was a swampy meadow and a tangle of brush surrounding some very large trees.

An Atlanta-based golf course architect, Cupp was on site for a layout walk-through in planning for what became Ghost Creek, one of two courses that would make up Pumpkin Ridge Golf Club. Cupp's associate at the time, John Fought, was there, along with founders Gay Davis, Marv French and Barney Hyde.

Davis had invited me to be on hand, and I had jumped at the opportunity. Then I watched as Cupp identified trees that had to be removed. At one point, Davis cringed and asked Cupp to explain why one particularly stately fir tree had to go.

"Because we have a green planned close by, and it won't get enough sun if the tree stays," Cupp said. Davis shook his head as if in surrender, and the tour continued.

It was an intriguing day for me, even if I couldn't visualize how the finished product would look. And I came away with a lot more respect for the skills of golf course architects.

"I've become enamored of this project," Cupp told me at the time. Later, after the final approval of regulatory agencies and with construction underway, he said, "I don't know of any project I've worked on that I was more sure would turn out just the way I envisioned."

The Safeway Classic, the Portland area's stop on the LPGA Tour, has drawn large galleries such as this one at Pumpkin Ridge's Ghost Creek course. *Courtesy of Tournament Golf Foundation.*

Thus it was that 350 acres of farmland west of Portland and near North Plains turned into a complex that soon would be acclaimed and selected to be host to national tournaments.

At first, the founders—operating under the name of Pumpkin Ridge Partners—planned for one eighteen-hole course. Cupp suggested that there be thirty-six holes. "We didn't want to compromise quality just to get thirty-six holes," Davis said. "Cupp assured us that wouldn't be the case."

So a second eighteen-hole course went onto the drawing boards, eventually to be named Witch Hollow. It was decided that Witch Hollow would be a private course, with Ghost Creek being available for public play. Cupp offered this observation about the par-five seventh hole at Witch Hollow (laid out at 620 yards from the back tee): "I've taken train rides shorter than that hole."

Fought, a former U.S. Amateur champion who grew up in the Portland area before winning two tournaments on the PGA Tour, laughed when asked about planning the project. "There were a few obstacles with the wetlands and such," he said. "We did thirteen plans before we had the one that was used."

Before the courses' bentgrass greens and fairways were even fully mature, *Golf Digest* selected Ghost Creek as the country's best new public course for 1992 and Witch Hollow as the number two new private course. Part of the attraction seemed to be that, from the outset, the courses didn't look new, instead taking on an older, traditional appearance.

Davis, French and Hyde made it clear from the start that they wanted golf courses that could compete to play host to major national events. That was their thinking from the time that Davis and French hatched the idea for the project.

"We talked about eventually being host to all thirteen of the U.S. Golf Association championships with the U.S. Open being the pinnacle," Davis said.

With Japanese investor Shigeru Ito becoming a fifty-fifty partner in the complex, the courses were opened for play in 1992. A mere thirty-three days after both were in operation, the USGA accepted the club's bid to be host to the 1996 U.S. Amateur. But the club was host to a national tournament even before that, the Nike (now Nationwide) Tour Championship in 1993. It was won by David Duval.

It snowballed from there with the U.S. Women's Open being staged in 1997 and 2003. In 2000, Pumpkin Ridge became the first club to stage the U.S. Junior Amateurs—boys and girls—simultaneously at the same site. The U.S. Women's Amateur followed in 2006. USGA officials were lavish in their praise of the club, the volunteers and the strong spectator support.

At the 1996 U.S. Amateur, in which Tiger Woods claimed his record third consecutive title before turning pro, then USGA executive director David Fay said, "There would be no downside to having a U.S. Open at Pumpkin Ridge." Judy Bell, then the USGA president, added, "Frankly, I could see Pumpkin Ridge hosting each of our championships over the course of time."

A year later, Fay, who retired at the end of 2010, said, "Pumpkin Ridge has a number of things going for it [in bidding for the Open]—the course, the infrastructure, the people involved and the golf community." Fresh in his mind were record crowds that had turned out at Witch Hollow to watch Alison Nicholas edge Nancy Lopez for the 1997 U.S. Women's Open crown.

Discussions went so far that USGA officials studied Pumpkin Ridge's two courses and determined that, with alterations, the Ghost Creek course would be best as an Open site. Contemplated alterations would have reduced the course's par to seventy and increased its maximum length from 6,950 yards to about 7,200 yards.

Former USGA executive director David Fay (left) and Gay Davis pose in 2011 after Davis's golf marathon fundraiser at Pumpkin Ridge netted $85,000 for the Children's Cancer Association. *Courtesy of Pacific Northwest GA.*

"But realistically, that is about as long as we could make it," Davis said. "We were sort of dropped out of the loop when the USGA decided that it wanted 7,500 yards."

Advanced technology of clubs and balls had dealt a major blow to the dreams and ambitions of Pumpkin Ridge's founders.

So instead of Pumpkin Ridge becoming the first club in the Pacific Northwest to be host to the Open, that honor went to Chambers Bay on Washington's Puget Sound, which was awarded the 2015 tournament. Chambers Bay, a links-style layout designed by Robert Trent Jones Jr., was host to the 2010 U.S. Amateur and can play to 7,585 yards.

So, Davis, French and Hyde—in partnership with former majority owner Ito's daughter Kumiko—continued to seek USGA national tournaments. Bids were in for the organization's Mid-Amateur and Senior Amateur. Meanwhile, Pumpkin Ridge has been host to the LPGA's Safeway Classic since 2009.

There were other contributions, such as Davis taking pledges and playing 108 holes in one day at Witch Hollow in the fall of 2011. To his delight, the fundraiser provided $85,000 for the Children's Cancer Association.

Davis, a two-time Oregon Amateur champion, admitted to frustration, though. He felt that the technology-improved ball was the culprit in creating a big problem in golf—courses once long enough to host major championships gradually becoming too short.

Gay Davis, one of the founders of the Pumpkin Ridge complex, kneels behind a youth representative of the Children's Cancer Association after Davis's 108-hole golf marathon. *Courtesy of Pacific Northwest GA.*

"Just cool off the ball, roll it back 2 percent [of distance] a year for five years," he said. "I don't think that would disrupt the game, and I really believe that gradual decrease would take care of the problem."

Then, he reasoned, maybe courses such as Pumpkin Ridge could again be in the running to stage a U.S. Open.

Chapter 16

TURMOIL AT SHOAL CREEK

Payne Stewart, the defending titlist, seemed to be his jovial self when he came to the media center for his pre-tournament news conference two days before the start of the 1990 PGA Championship. But he didn't get asked the usual questions about his game and the golf course, and his mood changed.

This was Shoal Creek Country Club, near Birmingham, Alabama, much maligned in preceding weeks after its founder, Hall Thompson, had made inflammatory racial comments to Joan Mazzolini of the *Birmingham Post-Herald.*

Mazzolini, who was gathering material for advance stories on the tournament, asked Thompson if his club had any African American members. He replied, "That's just not done in Birmingham. Bringing up this issue will just polarize the community, but it can't pressure us. The country club is our home, and we pick and choose who we want." Thompson later apologized, but the damage had been done.

There was instant reaction nationwide. It was hardly a secret that there was bigotry at many country clubs in the United States, but until Thompson made his indelicate comments, tournament producers and sponsors had conveniently ignored the problem. But it burst into the open at Shoal Creek, a club opened in 1977.

More than $2 million in advertising business was withdrawn for the ABC-TV and ESPN telecasts, and two civil rights groups, including the National Association for the Advancement of Colored People, announced plans to protest on-site.

Under pressure, the PGA announced that the tournament would be moved if Shoal Creek didn't loosen its membership requirements. The club did, inviting Louis Willie, an African American insurance executive, to become an honorary member. Plans for the protests were called off, and so was the PGA's threat to change venues.

As the late Stewart faced reporters and broadcasters that day in the media center, the PGA hoped the controversy would disappear from the limelight. It didn't.

Almost immediately, Stewart was asked about the racially charged situation. At first, he squirmed and said he didn't want to comment. But never one to hold back his thoughts on just about any subject, he then relented and said, "I think the players are making more jokes about this than anything else. I play golf for a living. I don't deal in policies. This thing is blown way out of proportion. You guys in the media are good at blowing things out of proportion. There's racism all over the world. Why single out this one incident?"

It was like fanning the flames for many of the more than seven hundred media representatives covering the Shoal Creek event. On this occasion, many were not there to write about the golf but to produce more stories on the controversy. So it turned into an eerie scene on the days preceding tournament play.

Many other players responded with varying degrees of cooperation. Jack Nicklaus, designer of the Shoal Creek course, said, "That's old news." Greg Norman said, "It's done. I don't want to talk about it." Even Fuzzy Zoeller, who seldom backs away from an interview question, said, "I think our job is to be down here to play golf. I don't have anything to do with politics."

I talked to Oregon pros Peter Jacobsen and Bob Gilder, and both were more cooperative in answering questions than many of their peers.

Jacobsen said, "We have no discrimination on our tour, and Calvin Peete [a black golfer] is one of our most dynamic leaders, a fellow who has done so much for inner-city youth programs. This is an issue that needs to be looked at carefully, but as a player, I don't have feelings one way or another."

Gilder said, "It is my understanding that a club has the right to have whomever it wants as members. There will be black players and black spectators here, so what's the big deal?"

Mostly, in the last two days before the tournament's opening round, those closest to the issue didn't want to talk about the situation. So I went looking for people who would talk to me.

Thompson declined to make himself available for interviews, and Shoal Creek members obviously had been advised not to comment. However, I found a member, Steve Coleman, who agreed to answer some questions. He said he felt that Shoal Creek had gotten an unfair rap in the days since Thompson made his comments.

"Unfortunately, a lot of misinformation has gone all over the country," he said. "It's very frustrating. The feelings that have been expressed in the media are not the feelings of the club as a whole. To my knowledge, the subject of having black members just never had come up. No blacks had applied, and I don't know of anyone in the club who discussed the matter."

I also talked to some African American caddies, including Herman Mitchell who was working for Lee Trevino. "I'm just here to work," Mitchell said. "I'm not into politics. I've been treated great here. Not just good, but great."

Behind the scenes, though, the PGA and other golf associations that conduct championship tournaments quickly changed rules so that they wouldn't schedule future tournaments at clubs that had discriminatory membership policies. In following months, announcements were made periodically about clubs opening their memberships to blacks, women (besides spouses of male members) and other minorities. Even Augusta National Golf Club, home of the Masters, accepted an honorary black member.

Oregonian Bob Gilder was among players feeling that the media overreacted to the controversy at the 1990 PGA Championship at Shoal Creek Country Club near Birmingham, Alabama. *Courtesy of Jeff Sanders Promotions.*

Anyway, the attention at Shoal Creek finally turned to golf. I'm sure that PGA officials hoped for a big-name winner to divert attention away from the controversy. Instead, it got little-known Australian Wayne Grady who had the tournament of his life and won by three shots over Fred Couples with Gil Morgan another stroke back.

The atmosphere seemed to get back almost to normal among the golfers as the tournament ran its course, and several of them complained about Shoal Creek's severely undulating greens and nasty Bermuda grass rough.

Zoeller, so reticent to speak about racial implications earlier in the week, unloaded this barb on the Shoal Creek course: "I have a lot of patience, but this course got on my nerves. Now we can get the hell out of town, and they can feed that rough to the cows."

In the years since 1990, Shoal Creek has added African American members and single women to its membership. Condoleeza Rice, secretary of state during the presidency of George W. Bush, became a member in 2009. Finally, in 2008, Shoal Creek was host to another national championship—the U.S. Golf Association's U.S. Junior Amateur.

The controversy and reaction at Shoal Creek in 1990 didn't come close to eliminating bigotry at country clubs coast to coast. But the attention certainly brought increased awareness of the problem. I think that, in turn, pushed golf in a better direction.

Chapter 17

TIGER AND HIS "A" GAME

Earl Woods, flamboyant father of budding golf star Tiger Woods, was moving slowly that day, recovering from triple-bypass heart surgery. He smiled a greeting and shook my hand, then said, "I better sit down. I'm still a little weak."

It was three weeks before the 1997 Masters tournament, and the elder Woods was in Portland on a speaking engagement for a bottling company. I had jumped at an offer to have lunch with him and others at Oregon Golf Club in West Linn.

Earl might have been short of energy, but he quickly showed that he hadn't lost his sense of humor. As the party of ten settled at a table in the private club's dining room, he noticed that the group included only three Caucasians. He grinned and said, "Now this is a situation we wouldn't have had a few years ago."

I had had previous visits with Woods on occasions when Tiger played in junior and amateur events in the Pacific Northwest, but I looked at this meeting as a chance to talk to him about his son's upcoming play in the Masters, his first major championship as a pro. I also hoped to get his views on Tiger's early impact on the game as a tour player.

Eventually, after I joined him briefly on the balcony where he went to smoke a cigarette, "against doctor's orders," we talked about Tiger, who already had claimed two tour wins late in the 1996 season.

"I'm not surprised at what he has accomplished," he said. "I knew what he had. The thing that has surprised me is that he has done it without his 'A' game. I don't know if anyone can beat him when he is playing his 'A' game."

Tiger Woods raises his arms in celebration after his comeback victory in the
1996 U.S. Amateur at Pumpkin Ridge's Witch Hollow course. He edged out
Steve Scott on the thirty-eighth hole. *Photo by Michael Lloyd/*Oregonian.

Then, as if to justify his braggadocio, he pointed out that I had seen that game twice. Those occasions were when Tiger won the Pacific Northwest Amateur in 1994 at Royal Oaks Country Club in Vancouver, Washington, and in the final round of the U.S. Amateur's title match in 1996 at Pumpkin Ridge's Witch Hollow course, west of Portland.

At Royal Oaks, when he was eighteen and playing in his first amateur tournament as an adult, Woods ignored a bad cold and was stunning on a course considered one of the most difficult in the area. He was thirty-five under par for 142 holes that week, counting both qualifying rounds and matches, and was thirteen under for 26 holes in the scheduled 36-hole final, crushing University of Oregon golfer and reigning Oregon Amateur champion Ted Snavely eleven and ten.

At Pumpkin Ridge, Woods struggled in the morning round of another thirty-six-hole final and found himself five-down to University of Florida golfer Steve Scott, who had shot a sixty-eight. Imagine Scott's consternation when he kept his poise for a bogey-free seventy in the afternoon and still saw his lead eliminated by Woods's seven-under sixty-five, which also included no bogeys. Woods then claimed his record third-consecutive Amateur title with a par on the thirty-eighth hole.

All of this came to mind while I was covering the Masters that spring and watching Woods obliterate the field and seemingly lay waste to the storied Augusta National Golf Club course. After Tiger's struggling front-nine forty in the opening round in windy conditions, I didn't need Earl there to point out to me that I again was seeing his son's "A" game.

It was extremely early in the tournament for a supposed telltale shot, but I thought I saw one as Tiger rallied for a back-nine thirty in that first round, giving him a two-under seventy, just three shots behind leader John Huston.

It came at the 500-yard fifteenth hole, the tantalizing par-five with a

The program cover for 1996 U.S. Amateur shows one of Pumpkin Ridge's clubhouses and the Amateur's trophy. *Courtesy of the author.*

pond in front of a wide green that is narrow in depth, especially on the left side, and has scary sloping back toward the water. Woods's drive was enormous down the right side, and he was left with only 151 yards to the pin, dangerously located far to the left.

I happened to be close enough to hear him tell caddie Mike Cowan that he was going to use a pitching wedge from the downhill lie. I swallowed in wonder. It looked as if, even for him, a nine-iron or a choked-up eight-iron to the middle of the green would have been the more rational play. Wouldn't there be a strong possibility of a pitching wedge shot sucking right back off the green? To me, using a wedge from that distance with a landing target about ten feet in diameter was golf in the twilight zone.

Then I watched in awe as Woods hit a towering shot that hung in the air like a soaring hawk before dropping almost straight down onto the green. The ball landed like a beanbag, stopping four feet from the cup. He sank the eagle putt, and the gallery's roar sent the kind of echo over the premises that usually was reserved for shots by Arnold Palmer and Jack Nicklaus.

What happened after that has been well chronicled. Woods went 65, 66 and 69 in the last three rounds, setting Masters records for low score (18-under-par 270) and largest margin of victory (twelve strokes). He led by three after the second round and by nine after the third.

After the second round, a few of his rivals offered brave words about possibly catching Woods. One was Colin Montgomerie, whose sixty-seven had moved him into second place. Of playing in a twosome with Woods in the third round, he said, "There is more to this than hitting the ball a long ways. The pressure is mounting on him more and more."

After shooting seventy-four to Woods's sixty-six the next day, a subdued Montgomerie said, "There is no chance, no human possibility, that Tiger Woods is going to lose this tournament."

Then there was the comment of six-time Masters champion Nicklaus. "I still can compete with everyone else in the field, but not with him."

Asked about Woods's talent, Nick Price said, "He can do things to a golf course that the rest of us just dream about."

The final round was strange in a way. There was no contest involved, with Woods's lead never sinking to fewer than eight shots. After finishing second at 282, Tom Kite said, "The best I could do was go out and try to win the silver medal."

Still, the scene was captivating as Woods went for his records and also became the first black golfer to don the coveted green jacket.

Lee Elder, the first black invited to play at Augusta in 1975, thought the occasion was special enough that he took a Sunday morning flight from Florida to join the gallery for Woods's final round.

"This win by Tiger has the potential to be even bigger than Jackie Robinson's breakthrough in baseball," Elder said. "No one will turn his head when a black man walks to the first tee after this."

Phil Knight, the Nike co-founder and an Oregon resident, was there following Woods that day and had trouble toning down his excitement. He also had a barb for critics who felt that Nike paid too much when it gave Woods an endorsement contract, the amount not announced but believed to have been between $35 and $40 million.

"The sports marketing world never has seen a pair like we have [Woods and Michael Jordan]," Knight said. "Some say we paid Tiger too much. I don't think so. We are very happy with our investment."

Now, looking back, I wonder how Earl Woods, who died in 2006, would have inserted himself when Tiger's personal life took a hit, starting late in 2009, with charges of infidelity followed by a much-publicized divorce from his wife, Elin. I also recall something else Earl said in our pre-Masters meeting in 1997 while talking about his son's impact on the game.

"Young players are coming up who will be outstanding," he said. "I don't know who they are, but I know they are there. When they surface, we'll just have to see what they have in their tanks, what kind of hearts they have."

It occurs to me that we now know some of those names—Luke Donald, Rory McIlroy, Bubba Watson, Dustin Johnson, Martin Kaymer, Hunter Mahan, Rickie Fowler, Adam Scott, Nick Watney, Keegan Bradley and Bill Haas, to name a few. When or if Tiger, who had won fourteen major championships going into 2012, recovers fully from knee and foot problems and the scandal, he most certainly will need what his father referred to as his "A" game to cope with their challenges.

Chapter 18

CASEY GOES TO COURT

The room was packed in the Federal Courthouse in Eugene, Oregon. Casey Martin sat at a table with his attorneys, a stoical look on his face. There was quiet anticipation and some impatience. The wait was on for U.S. Magistrate Thomas Coffin to enter and announce his verdict on Martin's suit to ride a golf cart in PGA and Nike (now Nationwide) Tour events.

I was in a row with other media members that February day in 1998, and I was convinced that the ruling would go in Martin's favor. It seemed to me that his attorneys, family friend Bill Wiswall and Martha Walters, a civil rights expert, had presented a solid case under guidelines of the Americans with Disabilities Act.

As we waited, I thought back on the difficult journey Martin had taken to play the game he loved at such a high level. I first watched him in an Oregon Junior tournament when he was eleven. I remembered how impressed I was with his fortitude in limping around the course, his right leg in obvious pain, and still playing well.

Later, I got to know Martin's brother Cam, and his parents, King and Melinda, well as Casey, playing for South Eugene, took medalist honors and also was on a title team in the Oregon High School Championships. Cam also was on that title team and had won a medalist trophy earlier.

After that, the two brothers went back-to-back in winning Oregon Amateur titles before Casey went on to Stanford, won the U.S. Intercollegiate tournament one year and played on an NCAA championship team in 1994, earning all-America mention. He also was on Stanford's runner-up team in 1995 when Tiger Woods was a teammate.

I also recalled the excitement when Martin made holes in one on back-to-back days at the 1994 Sunriver Oregon Open on the Central Oregon resort's Woodlands Course.

Then my attention came back to the weeklong trial that was about to conclude.

I felt that Wiswall and Walters had shown graphically, with a video and testimony, just how debilitating Martin's lifelong disability had become. The blood-disorder affliction, with the technical name of Klippel-Trenaunay-Weber Syndrome, had shriveled his right leg, and it had become so painful that he no longer felt able to walk a golf course on successive days of competition.

Amazingly, he had been able to continue playing well through constant pain and sleepless nights. Less than a month before, after Wiswall had succeeded in getting him a temporary injunction to ride in two Nike Tour tournaments, Martin won the first, the Nike Lakeland Classic in Florida.

At the same time, the PGA Tour's attorneys, headed by Bill Maledon, had come across as arrogant and insensitive. I also had the feeling that the tour

Casey Martin, shown here hitting a drive in 2011, made national news in 1998 with his successful lawsuit to ride a cart in PGA and Nationwide Tour tournaments. *Photo by Jon Ferry.*

hadn't made any points with Coffin when commissioner Tim Finchem told some writers, "It's troublesome that the person making the decision doesn't understand the situation."

The tour, conceding that Martin had a disability, hammered away that the case wasn't about him but only about the right of the tour as a private organization to make its own rules. It also claimed that Martin, riding a cart, would have an "unfair advantage" over rival golfers who had to follow the tour's no-cart rule for the PGA and Nike Tours.

Then it happened. Coffin, saying that the tour was wrong in not considering Martin as an individual and that it hadn't proven that the game would be altered by having Martin ride, ruled in the golfer's favor.

"Anyone who feels that Mr. Martin would have an unfair advantage by riding is wrong," Coffin said.

Martin's eyes watered, and he looked at the ceiling. Then he stood up and hugged Walters.

Later, Walters recalled the emotional exchange. She said, "All he said was, 'We won.' It was such an exciting moment."

Earlier, after one of the trial sessions, Martin looked frustrated when he said, "They keep saying this isn't about me, but it is about me."

Standing nearby, Wiswall smiled and said, "I've never represented a client and then had the other side say the case wasn't about my client."

The trial had been intriguing from the outset, and the national media was out in force. Media members had to check in the day before each trial session to arrange for seating.

The tour's attorneys brought in heavy artillery—including 1964 U.S. Open champion Ken Venturi and Richard Ferris, chairman of the nine-member PGA Tour Policy Board. Finchem testified, and there also were depositions from Arnold Palmer and Jack Nicklaus expressing their disapproval of Martin getting to ride. One of Palmer's comments—that if Martin got to ride, the PGA Tour might eventually disappear—came across as ludicrous.

Wiswall forced the opposition to watch a video of Martin's gruesome-looking leg (with the compression sock removed), a video he had sent to tour attorneys before the trial but that they had returned, the package unopened. He also did a good job of combating the testimony of Venturi and Ferris.

Venturi talked at length about playing his final round of the 1964 Open at Congressional Country Club with heat prostration but still walking. Wiswall countered by asking Venturi if he felt he had an unfair advantage when he was allowed by U.S. Golf Association officials to fall behind the group in front of him, or when he put his hand on the shoulders of USGA officials for support in approaching some greens.

Venturi begrudgingly admitted that maybe he had been cut some slack.

Wiswall asked Ferris if he walked while playing golf. He said that he did. Wiswall asked if any of his golfing friends rode carts. He said that they did. Wiswall asked if he thought that gave his friends an unfair advantage. Looking trapped, Ferris said he did not think so.

In his deposition, Nicklaus argued that the tour would be swamped with requests to ride from players with injuries or illnesses if the court ruled in favor of Martin. "How would you draw the line on which players would get carts?" he said.

Several other players, including Tom Watson and Fred Couples, had expressed similar views and said that they felt riding would give Martin an unfair advantage because he wouldn't have the same fatigue problems as walking players. Greg Norman, Tom Lehman, Bob Gilder and John Cook were among players supporting Martin's bid.

During his own testimony, Martin was asked by Maledon if he thought he had gotten an advantage from riding at the Tour Qualifying School or at the Lakeland tournament. "Absolutely not," he replied. "Hitting shots is what golf is all about. Walking is incidental to the game."

Martin also estimated that, even using a cart, he walked about one hundred yards per hole going to and from greens. "It's not that I don't walk at all [when playing out of a cart]."

What the tour and its supporting players refused to acknowledge was that, by riding, Martin simply was taking away some of the disadvantage he had because of his disability.

It seemed to me that the tour could have avoided a court case altogether by altering its rules on carts to allow a player with a lifelong disability to use a cart but not players with injuries or illnesses from which they had a chance to recover. The possibility obviously was miniscule that another player with a disabling ailment such as Martin's would become good enough to qualify for tour play.

Shortly after Coffin made his ruling, Maledon said that the tour would appeal the decision to a federal appeals court.

Then the story took on a new twist when Martin qualified to play in the 1998 U.S. Open at the Olympic Club near San Francisco. He did it in dramatic fashion in a sectional qualifier at Clovernook Country Club in Cincinnati, Ohio. I watched in awe of his poise as he rolled in a twenty-five-foot birdie putt on the second hole of a playoff and earned the final of five berths available.

The USGA, which followed the same rule against using carts in its major championships as the PGA Tour, observed the court's ruling and offered Martin a single-rider cart at the Olympic Club. It malfunctioned on the first hole of his first practice round and was replaced by a smaller, three-wheeler that nearly tipped over once before Martin abandoned it and began walking.

David Fay, then executive director of the USGA, was embarrassed and immediately ordered that a regulation cart be delivered to Martin.

Once the Open began, Martin and his cart posed no problem. A volunteer was assigned to walk along, and when Martin got out to go to a green, the volunteer would drive the cart to the vicinity of the next tee. Martin then would walk from the green to the next tee before resuming his cart ride.

The late Payne Stewart, who eventually finished second to Lee Janzen, shot sixty-six to lead after the Open's first round. When asked about Martin, he said, "This gentleman is handicapped, but he can play. The tour should have been bigger than it has been about this and recognized it as a special case."

Asked if he thought Martin gained an unfair advantage by riding, Stewart said, "I don't think Casey has an advantage over me. I think I still have an advantage over him."

Martin played well in the Open, drawing large followings. He shot an 11-over-par 291 and tied for twenty-third place, while Janzen was at an even-par 280 in winning. Statistics on driving distance for the sixty players making the cut had Martin in second place with a 291.3-yard average behind John Daly (295.6).

Martin then earned his PGA Tour card for the 2000 season, shortly before a federal appeals court refused to overturn Coffin's decision. The tour then appealed to the Supreme Court, which, in May 2001, ruled by a seven-to-two margin that Martin had a legal right to ride a cart in tour events.

Unfortunately for Martin, his tour play was hampered by further health issues and poor putting, and he eventually lost his playing card. His best finish in the 2000 season was a tie for seventeenth in the Tucson Open.

He became golf coach at the University of Oregon in 2006, maintaining his professional status and playing in selected events. The Ducks' program thrived under his leadership and began an upward climb in status. Martin even was named Pacific-Ten Conference coach of the year in 2010 when the Ducks made it to the NCAA Final Four.

All the while, he seemed content in the knowledge that the court rulings had given him the opportunity to, as he put it, "pursue my dream." Actually, that's what it was all about in the first place.

Chapter 19

PORTLAND'S LPGA BONANZA

Elon Ellis thought the idea would be a great one. Use bouquets of flowers as tee markers for an early Portland Classic, an LPGA Tour event at Portland Golf Club.

"They looked beautiful, and I was delighted," recalled Ellis, the tournament's founder. "I was delighted until the bees started swarming around the flowers and the players. Several players complained, some of them pretty loudly."

An embarrassed Ellis called for help, and the bouquets were removed as quickly as possible. Then he breathed a sigh of relief. "I guess I should have known better," he said.

Such was one of the bumps in the road for a tournament that blossomed into one of the tour's most successful and longest-lasting—forty years and counting through 2011—after its inaugural staging in 1972.

Another bump came in one of the early tournaments when Ellis, a Portland Golf Club member, promised to have Kathy Whitworth at a Downtown Rotary luncheon a couple days before the tournament's pro-amateur. "I was supposed to pick her up at the club, but she wasn't there," Ellis said. "Later, Kathy told me she just forgot. She felt terrible about it."

Anyway, Ellis was in panic mode and went looking for another player to take to the luncheon. "I went outside, and the only player I could find was Shelley Hamlin, who was in her first or second year on the tour," he said. "I said, 'Shelley, you're it.' She smiled and said that it was all right with her."

Tom Maletis, president of the management group for the LPGA's Safeway Classic, hugs Annika Sorenstam after one of her rounds at Columbia Edgewater Country Club. *Photo by Eric Yaillen/OGA.*

When Ellis and Hamlin arrived at the luncheon, Ellis got several disgusted looks from guests who were looking forward to hearing the highly acclaimed Whitworth and hadn't even heard of Hamlin.

"Then Shelley got up, and she wowed them," Ellis said. "She was the biggest hit you could imagine. Did I ever feel lucky."

Ellis, who died in 2003, got the idea for an LPGA event from memories of his membership in a group that called itself the "Trembling Twenty" and staged the Portland Open, a PGA Tour tournament, a few years earlier. Jack Nicklaus and Billy Casper were among the winners of that one.

"Elon had this idea for a women's tournament and convinced us to go along with him," said Bob Norquist, one of twenty-seven charter members of what was to become Tournament Golf Foundation. "We put up one hundred dollars each to get things started, and each of us had to go out and sell one hundred tickets. We hit up a lot of friends to get the tickets sold."

Those charter members swallowed their egos and divided up duties to get the tournament accomplished.

"I was tournament chairman the first two years," Norquist said. "The third year, I was in charge of portable toilets. That's kind of how the jobs were passed around. When something needed doing, a bunch of us would just get together and do it."

At the 1972 tournament, there weren't enough pros to fill up the fifty-team pro-amateur field. So two outstanding amateurs were recruited to play as "pros." One of them was 1972 U.S. Women's Amateur champion Mary Budke, and she helped her team to a second-place finish.

That on-the-fly first tournament had an overall purse of $25,000, and Whitworth, the tour's all-time leader in wins, earned $3,750 for her victory.

In 2011, as the Safeway Classic at Pumpkin Ridge Golf Club, the event had a purse of $1.5 million. Suzann Pettersen collected $225,000 as champion.

Tom Maletis, in his seventeenth year as TGF president and twenty-fourth year as a member of the event's all-volunteer management group, was quick to emphasize the importance of Ellis to what has followed.

"Elon gave us the foundation for a great tournament," he said. "We owed a lot to him because he set the stage for us."

The tournament's growth was steady with play at four Portland-area courses over the years—Portland Golf Club, Columbia Edgewater Country Club, Riverside Golf and Country Club and, finally, Pumpkin Ridge Golf Club. The annual pro-amateur grew to as many as 440 players with the use of Pumpkin Ridge's two courses. Attendance continued to climb in 2011, with a record tournament week turnout estimated at 88,100.

I remember Ellis telling me that only once in the early years was the event's future seriously in jeopardy. That was in 1980, when then PGA Tour commissioner Deane Beman came to Portland in hopes of selling TGF on switching its efforts to the staging of an event on the new Senior PGA Tour, now called the Champions Tour.

"He gave us quite a sales pitch," Ellis said. "He intimated that the senior pros would be better for us than the women, that the seniors would be more popular as pro-amateur participants. I have to admit that, at the time, there was kind of a magic about what he was selling."

But Ellis, a longtime officer of the Western Golf Association, said he couldn't turn his back on the LPGA, and with the approval of his fellow TGF members, he rejected Beman's offer.

The Portland tour stop has had several names along the way as title sponsors changed or joined

Jack Nicklaus is presented with the trophy for winning the 1965 Portland Open by Elon Ellis (center) and Charles Davis of the sponsoring Trembling Twenty group. *Courtesy of Ellis Family.*

forces—Ping Golf, Cellular One, AT&T Wireless Services and, finally, Safeway all have been a part of title sponsorships. From 1977 to '82, it was a team tournament with partners using a best-ball format. As the Portland event has grown, so has its management group—to thirty-nine members going into 2012.

Maletis pointed to Safeway's sponsorship, which began in 1996, as pivotal to the long-term success, especially in the group's contributions to its children's charities—more than $16 million over forty years.

"It has been such a good fit because we are on the same page as the Safeway people," Maletis said. "They understand our goals, and they really care about our charities."

Perhaps partially because of the challenging nature of the courses used, the Classic often has been won by some of the game's most storied players—Whitworth, JoAnne Carner, Donna Caponi, Nancy Lopez, Amy Alcott, Betsy King, Patty Sheehan, Dottie Pepper, Juli Inkster, Annika Sorenstam and Lorena Ochoa, to name the most prominent.

A crowd surrounds the eighteenth green at Pumpkin Ridge's Ghost Creek course during the final round of the 2011 Safeway Classic. *Courtesy of Tournament Golf Foundation.*

Exciting finishes? There have been many.

Lopez won two of her four titles in playoffs. She sank a five-foot birdie putt on the second extra hole to beat Lori Garbacz in 1985 at Riverside and won with a par on the third extra hole over Jane Crafter in 1992 at Columbia Edgewater.

King was three under par for her final five holes to score a one-stroke win over Colleen Walker in 1988 at Riverside.

Muffin Spencer-Devlin's tee shot at Riverside's sixteenth hole in the final round was headed for water in 1989 when it struck a spectator's foot and stayed dry. She made a par on the hole and went on to win by one stroke over four players, including home-state pro Susan Sanders of Salem.

Sheehan's one-shot win over Danielle Ammaccapane in 1990 featured a twenty-foot birdie putt at Columbia Edgewater's eighteenth hole, giving her a closing sixty-seven. Her goal that day had been to shoot her father BoBo's age (sixty-eight) on his birthday. "I think he will forgive me for beating it by one," she said.

Sorenstam delighted spectators with back-to-back victories at Columbia Edgewater in 2002 and 2003. A course-record sixty-two in the second round sent Sorenstam on her way to victory in 2002, but she had to sink an eleven-foot birdie at the final hole to hold off late-charging Kate Golden by one stroke. Golden shot a day's best sixty-five and also made a birdie at the last hole.

When it came to national exposure, though, Inkster's six-shot win in 1999, a victory that clinched her spot in the LPGA Hall of Fame, took the prize. She was beaming as she walked up the eighteenth fairway at Columbia Edgewater. She waved to acknowledge applauding spectators. Next to the green, a large group of her fellow golfers waited impatiently for her to wrap up her victory.

Impressing me as much as anything was that Karrie Webb, who entered the Hall in 2005, was in the waiting group that day. She had missed the cut the day before but delayed her departure plans from Portland just to be there in case Inkster maintained her third-round lead for the pivotal win. "I stayed around because this is so special," she said.

Bob Norquist, here presenting junior golf awards, is one of the original members of Tournament Golf Foundation, management group of Portland's LPGA tournament. *Photo by Eric Yaillen/OGA.*

After Inkster putted out for her fifth win of a banner season, she was doused with champagne by a congratulating group that included Lopez and Beth Daniel, two other Hall of Fame members.

"Not in my wildest dreams did I think this would happen to me," said a teary-eyed Inkster, who won the 1981 U.S. Women's Amateur a few miles away at Waverley Country Club.

"To be part of that was pretty cool for all of us," Norquist said.

Chapter 20

DISCOVERING BANDON DUNES

John Conrad, sports editor of the *Eugene Register-Guard* for eighteen years before his death in 2002, grew up in the small town of Bandon on the Oregon coast. He was a star athlete in multiple sports at Bandon High School and went on to earn three varsity letters as a baseball pitcher for the University of Oregon.

In the latter capacity, he once struck out Reggie Jackson of Arizona State three times in one game. Not the least bit egotistical, he laughed and said of that experience, "It would have been more impressive if Reggie's teammates hadn't bombed me, and we hadn't lost big."

Conrad and I became good friends over the years and frequently played golf together. After one of our rounds, shortly before the Bandon Dunes Resort opened in May 1999 with its first course, Conrad laughed and gave me a scolding look when I asked what he thought of the project.

"There's no way that is going to work," he said. "Not enough population down there. Too far to drive to get there for most people."

I thought of Conrad and his evaluation on Bandon Dunes's opening day when 154 of 160 scheduled golfers showed up to play in miserable, rainy weather.

When he awoke that morning and saw the weather conditions, even owner Mike Keiser admitted to a sinking feeling. He thought to himself, "Only about half the people with tee times will show up. Maybe no one will show up."

I was there that day, not to play but to interview players about their impressions for a golf column I planned to write.

Owner/founder Mike Keiser (left) and two of his golf course architects, Tom Doak (center) and Jim Urbina, take a break from a tour of Bandon Dunes Resort courses. *Photo by Wood Sabold.*

The scene captivated me. Keiser and Josh Lesnik, the course's first general manager, greeted each foursome on the first tee and passed out commemorative medallions.

Later, when players finished, many soaked from the rain, I couldn't find anyone who had anything bad to say about the course or the experience. It was amazing, or so it seemed to me at the time.

"I've played in Scotland and Ireland, and this was like playing a course with the best holes from over there," said Gary Rothenberger.

"This is as good as anything I saw on trips to Scotland and Ireland," said Reid Hutchins.

"I think it is better than Pebble Beach," said Steve Stadum.

"I would call it a thrilling addition for golf on the Oregon coast," said actor Gregory Harrison, who had a home in nearby Gold Beach.

Late in the day, Keiser approached me and asked if I would like to play nine holes with him. I told him I would get back to him in a couple minutes. I looked up Lesnik and asked if Keiser had felt obligated to make such an offer. I didn't want to take him up on it if that was the case.

"Are you kidding?" Lesnik said. "Mike absolutely loves to play golf. He is dying to be out there. I'm sure he asked you because it would give him an excuse to go play."

So Keiser and I played nine holes in the rain, and he seemed to love every minute. I know I did, especially when I made a par on a par-three hole on which Keiser had his own elevated tee built on a dune away from the regular tee.

That's how it began for a golf resort that has become famous, drawing visitors from all over the world. Now, in 2012, there are four courses—Bandon Dunes, Pacific Dunes (opened in 2001), Bandon Trails (2005) and Old Macdonald (2010). In the fall of 2011, all four were ranked among the top one hundred courses in the United States by *Golf Magazine*, and the Bandon Dunes Resort was selected by *Golf Digest* as the number one golf resort in North America.

In addition, a short course with thirteen par-three holes was in the works, and there also was talk of perhaps building another eighteen-hole course.

Providing variety has been a prime goal of Keiser. While Bandon Dunes and Pacific Dunes have many of their holes hugging the coastline, Bandon Trails is inland with some of the characteristics of Augusta National.

How did such a thing happen? Bandon is hardly a metropolis, with a population that hovers at about three thousand. Its current economy revolves

The fourteenth hole of Bandon Dunes's Old Macdonald Course, shown here, is typical of the layout that has become one of the resort's most popular. *Photo by Wood Sabold.*

The first hole at Bandon Trails, one of the Bandon Dunes Resort's four eighteen-hole courses, features imposing mounds of rock and sand on the way to the green. *Photo by Wood Sabold.*

around wood products, fishing, tourism and agriculture. It is known for its cranberries, with more than one hundred growers and approximately 1,600 acres. Cheese making, once a primary business, is no longer, but "Bandon Cheese" is still available through the Tillamook Creamery Association. And the Bandon Dunes Resort ranks among the top five employers in the area.

It may come as a shock to some, but this amazingly successful development, drawing golfers from every country imaginable, came about almost by accident.

Keiser, an avid golfer living in Chicago, had huge success with his greeting-card business and decided he wanted to build his "dream golf course." He began looking for sites, first in Washington, D.C., and then North Carolina, South Carolina and Georgia. Nothing struck his fancy.

He started out wanting a coastal site but had just about given up on finding one. Then Howard McKee, a former Oregonian and one of Keiser's partners, mentioned to him that Oregon's climate is similar to that in North Carolina. The search headed west, and Keiser looked at possible sites in Northern California and in the Brookings area in Oregon.

Finally, Annie Huntamer, a Gold Beach real estate broker, heard of Keiser's interest and informed him of the property available just north of Bandon.

"When I saw the land, I knew right away that I had found the spot," Keiser said.

When a media day was held shortly before the opening of Pacific Dunes, I was paired to play in a group with John Conrad. Of course, I kidded him again about his earlier pessimism. He smiled and shook his head. I think he still was trying to figure out how he could have been so wrong.

Conrad had a stroke and died the next year, a shock because he was just fifty-seven. I can't help but wonder what he would think of Bandon Dunes now.

Chapter 21

RYDER CUP EMOTIONS

Peter Jacobsen had a bit of a chip on his shoulders when he arrived in Rochester, New York, for the 1995 Ryder Cup matches. How could it have been otherwise after he read *Sports Illustrated*'s evaluations of the two sides? He was described as the worst player on the United States team.

"Nice guys finish last," the *Sports Illustrated* evaluations said of the Portland pro. "Too soft to stick it to the likes of Seve (Ballesteros)."

On top of that, *Golf World*—in a capsule previewing the matches—listed Jacobsen's "defining moment" as a six-iron shot into a hazard on the final hole that cost him the title in the 1988 Western Open. Ignored were his two 1995 tournament wins that had earned him a spot on the U.S. team.

Anyway, I anticipated that he would be on the hot side when I first tracked him down at Oak Hill Country Club early in the week. He tried to make light of the magazine slights before admitting that he "kind of blew up" about them at the previous week's B.C. Open.

"I told off a *Golf World* reporter in front of a lot of people," he said. "It made the papers up there."

Then, smiling, he said that he would love to have a showdown with Spaniard Ballesteros sometime during the matches' three-day run. "I would welcome the chance to play him," he said.

Looking back, it struck me as a fine chance, through a description of Jacobsen's experiences in the 1995 matches, to illustrate the roller-coaster emotional ride that players take in the Ryder Cup.

The competition has heated up in recent years to the point that media interest is as high as it is for any of the four major championships. The pressure becomes immense on the players as they represent their country and seek to not let down teammates. Even easygoing Fred Couples was on edge in 1995. "It's nerve-wracking," he said. "I even get an upset stomach in the practice rounds."

U.S. Captain Lanny Wadkins had Jacobsen, along with three others, sit out the first round of matches on opening day as the Americans and Europeans went two and two in four alternate-shot matches. Then Jacobsen's dream came true. He and Brad Faxon would pair up against Ballesteros and David Gilford in an afternoon best-ball match. And his dream turned into a nightmare.

One of Peter Jacobsen's golfing strengths is his jovial disposition, which he shows here, laughing at a fellow player's comment. *Photo by Tom Treick.*

Jacobsen and Faxon started well enough, Jacobsen making two early birdies, and the match was even through six holes. Then disaster struck at the par-four seventh.

Faxon's tee shot caught the edge of a water hazard. But some willow trees blocked Jacobsen's view, and he didn't see Faxon take a penalty drop. A few minutes later, Faxon faced a fifteen-foot putt for a bogey on the same line as Jacobsen would be chipping for a birdie. Faxon made the putt before Jacobsen chipped three and one-half feet past the cup.

Jacobsen, thinking Faxon's putt had been for a par, walked onto the green and picked up his ball. "Nice four," he said to his partner. "That was a five, not a four," Faxon said.

Stunned, Jacobsen watched, glassy-eyed, as Ballesteros and Gilford won the hole with a par for a one-up lead. "When Brad told me that he had made a five, it hit me like a Muhammad Ali punch," Jacobsen said. "I felt so stupid about it."

Jacobsen and Faxon were unable to regroup and lost the match four and three. It wasn't a huge consolation to them, either, that their American teammates won the other three afternoon matches to give the United States a five-to-three lead.

After his teammates did their best to cheer him up at a team dinner that night, Jacobsen found it difficult to shake the downer he was on from his mistake.

"It meant so much to me to have the guys behind me like that," he said. "I got pretty emotional."

He also urged Wadkins to have him in the lineup for the next morning's alternate-shot matches. His request was granted. He would pair with Loren Roberts against Europeans Ian Woosnam and Philip Walton. Then he spent a restless night.

"I woke up and checked the clock at 12:50, 2:35, 4:00, 4:21 and 4:52," he said. "I couldn't wait to try and make up for yesterday."

Jacobsen and Roberts had their hands full against Woosnam and Walton, especially after Woosnam's birdie at the eleventh hole gave the European pair a one-up lead. Jacobsen's iron approaches to inside ten feet at the twelfth and thirteenth set up birdie putts by Roberts, and the Americans went in front to stay.

It got harrowing, though, at the difficult par-four eighteenth as they tried to maintain their one-up lead. Roberts pushed his drive into deep rough, and a nasty lie gave Jacobsen no chance to reach the elevated green with the second shot.

Peter Jacobsen's golf swing, always fundamentally sound, has helped him to seven wins on the PGA Tour and two victories in Champions Tour majors. *Photo by Tom Treick.*

"Loren told me to look down the fairway about sixty-five yards short of the green," Jacobsen said. "He pointed out a brown spot and told me to hit the ball there, and he would take care of getting it close [to the pin] for me."

Jacobsen slashed the ball out, and it settled a few feet from the brown spot. Then Roberts, true to his word, lofted a sand-wedge approach to within thirty inches of the cup, setting up Jacobsen's par putt that clinched the duo's one-up victory.

"I feel as if I got the point back that I lost yesterday," Jacobsen said. His eyes sparkled, extreme elation and relief showing.

The point earned by Jacobsen and Roberts was the lone one for the Americans that morning as they fell into a six-to-six tie. With Jacobsen being held out in the afternoon, the

United States won three of four best-ball matches to go back ahead nine to seven.

Then the United States had a singles flameout on the final day as the Europeans rallied to claim victory fourteen and one-half to thirteen and one-half. Included was Jacobsen's one-up loss to Howard Clark, who made a hole in one at the eleventh to even the match. Clark survived three Jacobsen birdies to take his first lead at the sixteenth. The final two holes were halved with pars.

Jacobsen was disappointed and frustrated, but it was nothing like his letdown two days earlier. He watched from a hillside next to the eighteenth green as three of his teammates—Faxon, Curtis Strange and Jay Haas—all made bogeys at the final hole to lose matches one-up. He felt their pain.

But when it was over, he was one of the few American players to go onto the green and congratulate the celebrating Europeans.

"Let's not forget, the Ryder Cup is not just about winning and losing," Jacobsen said. "It's about great golf and showcasing the accomplishments of twenty-four players. It's about the enjoyment and excitement that have developed in the United States and Europe over the matches and over golf in general."

His experiences, though, illustrated just how high and how low players' emotions can run in the Ryder Cup.

Chapter 22

SHIFTING GOLF GEARS

Jeff Sanders arrived at the Greater Milwaukee Open in September 1985 shaking off a case of the flu. He probably would have called in his withdrawal except that he was desperately trying to earn enough money to keep his PGA Tour card for 1986.

"I didn't get there until the day before the first round and too late for a practice round," he said. "I also had trouble lining up a caddie. The only one I could find was a bearded fellow named Larry. He walked with a limp, and he claimed he had worked for Billy Casper, among others." Later, Sanders would learn that he also had a suspect past.

Sanders, who grew up in Beaverton, west of Portland, was in his fifth year on tour, and things hadn't gone as well as he had anticipated. After all, he had considerable success as an amateur, including an Oregon Junior title and a pair of district championships for Sunset High School. At the University of Oregon, he earned all-American honors by finishing third at the 1976 NCAA Championship as a sophomore, the best-ever NCAA finish by a Duck. One of his teammates that season was future PGA Tour and Champions Tour player Peter Jacobsen of Portland.

As a pro, Sanders had won the Victoria Open on the tour subsidiary Tournament Players Series, earning his largest check for golf play—$36,000. He advanced through the Tour Qualifying School four times. "I got my card four times and then gave it back four times," he said.

When he arrived in Milwaukee, he figured his career might be on the line. Despite having a good year in earnings overall, including $55,000 on the Tournament Players Series, only about $25,000 of his earnings had come from official PGA Tour events. He was headed to finishing out of the top 150 in money for the year and losing his card again.

So, as he teed it up in Milwaukee that week, he didn't expect a miracle, but he hoped for one.

Then an amazing thing happened. His game came together, and with rounds of sixty-eight and sixty-seven, he was tied for the lead with Jim Colbert. Larry's limp made him lag behind, and Sanders said he "worried constantly" that he would be penalized for slow play. But admittedly superstitious to a fault, he declined to make a caddie change after such a good start even though Larry was causing him stress.

A seventy in the third round left him second behind Jim Thorpe and set up a final-round pairing with Thorpe and Jack Nicklaus.

When Sanders finished putting practice on the day of the final round and reported to the first tee, he had temporary panic. He couldn't find Larry, who had all of his clubs except the putter. Finally, Larry appeared, and Sanders noticed that Nicklaus gave the caddie a funny look.

As it turned out, Larry had approached Nicklaus in the parking lot early in the week claiming to be a cousin who needed money from his "relative." He didn't get it.

Nicklaus didn't tell Sanders about this until they had a slight delay on the third tee. "I couldn't help but laugh when Jack told me the story," Sanders said. "Actually, it helped to relax me."

Despite bogeys on the first two holes, Sanders fought back to be even-par on the front nine. But he followed with a forty-one on the back nine and wound up in a tie for fifteenth, earning $4,800.

"If I had shot par-thirty-six on the back nine, I would have tied Nicklaus for second place behind Thorpe and would have earned enough money to clinch my tour card for 1986," he said.

Instead, Sanders went on to finish 153rd on the money list and lost his card. "It's tough to be 153rd in the country in your field and be unemployed," he said.

Rather than returning to the Tour Qualifying School, Sanders decided to find himself another career in golf. He worked with Jacobsen and co-founder Mike Stoll on the first Fred Meyer Challenge in 1986 and then was hired by Norm Daniels, a GI Joe's Sporting Goods store executive, to manage the 1987 GI Joe's Northwest Open.

"I really appreciated the opportunity that Norm gave me, and I enjoyed the experience more than I thought I would," Sanders said. "It gave me the bug to branch out in that field."

So he took a big step and formulated a plan to have his own management company for sports, especially golf. Called Jeff Sanders Promotions, it was opened for business in 1989 with the home office in Beaverton. The GI Joe's/Thriftway Northwest Open that year was its first big event.

Sanders's firm concentrated on managing professional golf tournaments and corporate fundraising events. "I found a passion for the management end, similar to the passion I had for playing golf," he said.

The business blossomed. The Albertsons Team Championships, a made-for-TV event involving teams of men and women from golf clubs throughout the West, was started in 1989 and is ongoing. The Ben Hogan Boise Open (now called the Albertsons Boise Open on the Nationwide Tour) was taken over in 1990 and is ongoing. The GI Joe's/Thriftway Portland Invitational was conducted in 1993–99.

Sanders's firm also was the management group for the 1996 U.S. Amateur and the 1997 U.S. Women's Open, U.S. Golf Association championships played at Pumpkin Ridge Golf Club, west of Portland. Then came a series of charity tournaments, many in other parts of the country. The Winn-Dixie Jacksonville Open on the Nationwide Tour was added in 2010, and the Wheaties Pro-Amateur at Spyglass Hill, a part of the Champions Tour's First Tee Open, joined the fold in 2011.

Jeff Sanders (left) introduces guest Arnold Palmer at a pre-tournament clinic of the Albertsons Boise Open, a Nationwide Tour event that Sanders's company manages. *Courtesy of Jeff Sanders Promotions.*

Meanwhile, Sanders has become strictly a recreational golfer, albeit a good one. He regained his amateur standing in 1995 and, as of early in 2012, had a handicap of plus-one. His last tournament of consequence was the 1996 U.S. Amateur, at which he was tournament director. With rounds of seventy-one and seventy-four, he qualified for match play but then lost his first-round match.

"Playing in the Amateur that year was something I really wanted to do," he said. "It seemed especially cool when the USGA people told me that I was the first tournament director to play in the tournament."

Now with a staff of twenty at Jeff Sanders Promotions, he has found the kind of success that eluded him on the PGA Tour. It also has made it so that he doesn't look back on his tour career with regrets.

"Actually, I'd say that getting into the business I'm in has been the best thing that ever happened to me," he said. He even looks back and finds amusement in talking about some of things that happened to him in his previous career as a competitive golfer.

In the 1976 Northwest Open at Columbia Edgewater Country Club, his scorer wrote down his first-nine total of thirty-nine in the space reserved for the ninth hole score on his scorecard. He didn't catch the error and had to accept the thirty-nine instead of the par-four that he actually made. "I got a big lesson on scorekeeping that day," he said.

In the final round of the 1983 Giusti Memorial tournament at Columbia Edgewater, he hit the pin with his tee shot at the par-three eighth hole, nearly making a hole in one. Then, incredibly, he missed the birdie putt of barely more than a foot. He finished second, two shots behind Pat Fitzsimons. "I can't remember another time that I missed a putt that short," he said at the time.

As for Larry, his pickup caddie at Milwaukee, Sanders doesn't remember his last name, but he'll never forget him.

Chapter 23

FLASHBACK TALES

Portland Golf Club, mentioned prominently in several chapters of this book, seemed to develop a magic of sorts going back to its early days. Its lure showed in the large number of big tournaments that were played out on its tree-lined fairways, some with national and international flavor.

Located in the Raleigh Hills section west of Portland, the club was opened for play in 1914 with nine holes, designed by founding members. A second nine was ready in 1915 with the complex located on 137 acres. Some remodeling followed.

As the years passed and the course was improved, its subtle changes in elevation and its slick putting surfaces made it increasingly attractive for tournament play. Sam Snead, Ben Hogan, Billy Casper and Jack Nicklaus won Portland Open titles there, and Cary Middlecoff claimed a Western Open crown in 1955 with a final-round sixty-three.

In 1969, Casper got another victory at Portland Golf Club in the Alcan Golfer of the Year Championship, capitalizing on Lee Trevino's collapse over the final three holes. Miller Barber was the surprise winner when the U.S. Senior Open was staged in 1982. Later, some of the game's biggest names visited in the Peter Jacobsen–hosted Fred Meyer Challenge. The club also was host to a U.S. Senior Amateur and several regional championships.

On the women's side, the 1931 Western Amateur and the 1934 Western Open were contested there. Then Kathy Whitworth, Donna Caponi and Nancy Lopez scored wins on the course in the early days of Portland's LPGA tournament, now called the Safeway Classic.

But the plums of Portland Golf Club's past came with the 1946 PGA Championship and the 1947 Ryder Cup matches. In the former, Hogan defeated Ed "Porky" Oliver six and four in a scheduled thirty-six-hole final. Then, a year later, Hogan was playing captain of a United States team that crushed Great Britain/Ireland eleven to one in the Ryder Cup. Hogan had a pair of noteworthy honorary captains, too—Walter Hagen and Craig Wood.

Finally, in another history-making development, the Golf Writers Association of America was created at Portland Golf Club in meetings at the time of the 1946 PGA Championship.

CALLING A BLUFF

After amateur golfer Kent Myers returned from missing the cut in the 1956 U.S. Open at Oak Hill in Rochester, New York, the pro at his home Salem Golf Club—Gene "Bunny" Mason—kidded him about his "mediocre" rounds of eighty and eighty-one.

Myers bristled and said, "If you think I'm so bad, why don't you get your sticks, and we'll go out and play?" Mason took him up on it, and Myers made birdies on the first seven holes.

A few days later—in a weekly column he did briefly for the Salem, Oregon *Statesman*—Mason wrote, "Kent literally took the hide off my wallet."

Myers's play against Mason that day wasn't as miraculous as it might have seemed. He often played the 6,203-yard course with a par of seventy-two as if it had been designed for his personal pleasure. One day, he played twenty-seven consecutive holes in twenty-nine, thirty-three and twenty-nine.

With the trophy in his hands, a smiling Kent Myers celebrates after winning the 1994 Pacific Northwest Masters-Forty title. *Courtesy of Pacific Northwest GA.*

BEN'S WAY

The first time I watched Ben Crane play golf extensively was back in his college days at the University of Oregon. I was impressed the most by his bulldog tenacity as a competitor and with the confidence he had around the greens. Seemingly, there was no putt that he didn't think he could make, and I saw him make a bunch of them.

So, after he turned pro and earned his PGA Tour card, I looked deeper into his background. I learned that he got started in the game by his grandfather when he was five and that his fierce determination established stronger roots when he was thirteen and turned to then Portland Golf Club teaching pro Rick Lamberton for help.

"That first year, I'd never seen anyone with the work ethic Ben had," Lamberton said. "I remember one day, it was thirty-six degrees, and there was a mixture of rain and snow. Ben was out on our range in a golf shirt, hitting ball after ball. I knew then that he was something special."

Later, when Lamberton told him he needed to improve his putting, Crane frequently practiced on Portland Golf Club's lighted putting green long after dark, sometimes to the annoyance of the club's security officer.

When Crane was sixteen, he asked Lamberton if he had a chance to become a tour pro. "I told him that I thought that he could," Lamberton said.

Crane, improving steadily, went on to win the Pacific Coast Amateur and the Pacific Northwest Amateur and was a three-time all-Pacific-Ten Conference selection for the Ducks. When he turned pro, the steady improvement continued. When he realized that he needed more length off the tee, he turned to instructor Carl Welty for help. "The whole thing was about clubhead speed," he said. "I knew, if I was going to compete at the level I wanted, I had to have more of it, and I got it."

Now Crane is a successful PGA Tour pro who had won four times through the 2011 season. His workaholic nature hasn't changed, and his putting stroke still has its moments of magic.

PUZZLING CAREER

As a seventeen-year-old amateur, Pat Fitzsimons won the 1968 Oregon Open, outdueling pros Bob Duden and Al Feldman in a rain-plagued, thirty-six-hole final day at Astoria Golf and Country Club. A year later, still as an amateur, he won the Northwest Open at Inglewood Country Club in Kenmore, Washington. His ball-striking in those days was close to perfection, his putting deadly. One day, at his home Salem Golf Club, he shot an incredible fourteen-under-par fifty-eight. "It was as near as I'll come to a perfect round," he said a few years later. "I didn't miss a putt under fifteen feet."

Chuck Milne, later a club and teaching pro in the Portland area, grew up playing golf with Fitzsimons in Salem. "One day, Pat gave me a stroke on each nine for a game," he said. "I shot a 64 and lost. Pat had a 60."

Fitzsimons qualified for his PGA Tour card in 1971 and, in 1975, won the Los Angeles Open at Riviera Country Club. In the U.S. Open that year at Medinah Country Club in Illinois, he contended into the final round before tying for ninth behind winner Lou Graham. At the time, I thought he was on his way to becoming a top-tier tour player.

Instead, Fitzsimons's career hit the wall. Less than enamored with the tour life, he played less on the tour instead of more at a time when his confidence was at a peak. Then his putting touch deserted him, his confidence wavered and he lost his tour card. Turning to life as a club and teaching pro, he continued to win regional events, including two more Northwest Opens, another Oregon Open and three Pacific Northwest PGA Championships, but he never regained the level of play that he displayed in that banner 1975 season when he finished twentieth on the tour money list.

"I wasn't prepared for the stress of the tour," he told me later in self-analysis. "The better I did, the more expectations I had and the more pressure I applied to myself when I didn't meet those expectations."

DISTAFF DANDIES

In 2005, Marcia Fisher was profiled by *Golfweek* magazine in a "Local Legends" feature for her longtime excellence in women's amateur golf. About the same time, Joan Edwards-Powell appeared in *Sports Illustrated*'s "Faces in the Crowd" page for her many accomplishments in the sport.

"I never have thought of myself as a legend," Fisher said with a smile in reaction to her honor. In an earlier interview, she told me, "I'm kind of a ho-hum person, really. I just love to play the game."

Marcia Fisher shows a determined look on a shot in a 2009 tournament. Among her many wins have been seven Oregon Amateur titles. *Photo by Eric Yaillen/OGA.*

Edwards-Powell tends to be an open book about the game. "Golf is the study of a lifetime," she said. "You never can conquer it. The carrot always is dangling. You can exhaust yourself, but never your subject."

Both women, meshing their golf with family and career demands, have won a multitude of state and regional amateur tournaments and have been honored by the Pacific Northwest Golf Association and the Oregon Golf Association.

Joan Edwards-Powell is all smiles after earning a trophy in a 2010 amateur tournament. Twelve Women's Championships in the Oregon Coast Invitational are a career highlight. *Photo by Eric Yaillen/OGA.*

Fisher, from Willamette Valley Country Club in Canby, is a seven-time winner of the Oregon Amateur, among her many titles. Only 1972 U.S. Women's Amateur champion Mary Budke is ahead of her, with eight Oregon Amateur wins.

Edwards-Powell, who has spent most of her career playing out of Portland's Columbia Edgewater Country Club, has won the Oregon Coast Invitational at Astoria Golf and Country Club a stunning twelve times, rivaling the feats of Ralph Dichter in men's play at the same event. She also has claimed nine Oregon Golf Association championships in various divisions.

It seems that calling their feats legendary is no stretch at all.

LUCKY GUESS

I wandered out to watch action on the driving range early in the week of the 1970 U.S. Amateur at Waverley Country Club, southeast of Portland. I wasn't familiar with too many of the players and was planning to get a look at a few of them. I immediately spotted defending champion Steve Melnyk.

Not far from him was a little fellow with a short backswing and a quick move at the ball. He was hitting a long iron (I later learned that it was a three-iron) and was aiming at a two-hundred-yard sign. I watched as, on three consecutive shots, his ball took one bounce and banged off the sign. He then barely missed the sign with a couple of shots before hitting it twice more.

I turned to a nearby friend and said, "I don't know that guy's name, but I think he is going to win the tournament."

"That guy" was Lanny Wadkins, and he indeed won, edging Tom Kite by one shot in seventy-two holes of medal play, a 1-under-par 279 to 280. Shortly after that, the tournament was switched back to match play.

Wadkins, a twenty-year-old Wake Forest University junior at the time, did it in style, too, sinking a twenty-foot birdie putt on the final hole before Kite knocked in a ten-footer for a birdie that kept him one stroke back.

It was a watershed moment for the little fellow with the deadly three-iron. Among those he left in his wake that week, in addition to Kite and Melnyk, were Tom Watson, Ben Crenshaw, Gary Cowan, Vinny Giles, Andy North, Bill Campbell and Jay Sigel.

FAMILY AFFAIR

It's safe to say that George Mack had no idea what he was starting when he first entered the Oregon Coast Invitational more than fifty years ago. Now seventy-two, he looks back at one of the great stories of family-affair golf. When host Astoria Golf and Country Club celebrated the tournament's history-making 100th anniversary in 2010, the Mack family had laid claim to an amazing twenty championships in the event.

Mack, a longtime Portland accountant, had won four Grand Championships and three Senior Division titles. Son George Jr. had claimed three Grand Championships. Daughter Lara Tennant had won seven Women's Championships. Daughter Cappy Gray had captured two Women's Championships. Daughter Renee Baumgartner had won one Women's Championship.

In 2008, Tennant beat Gray in the women's title match. Father George loaded their clubs on a cart and proudly caddied for both players. "That was some kind of highlight for me," he said.

ABOUT THE AUTHOR

The gentleman's name was Ralph Kletzing. He was owner and publisher of the *Independence Enterprise*, a weekly newspaper in the small Oregon city west of Salem. He and his wife, Dorothy, were good friends of Bob Robinson's parents, Paul and Alice Robinson, and the couples frequently got together to play bridge on Saturday nights.

It was on one of those Saturday nights in August 1946 that a bridge game was going on in the Robinson household while Bob was nearby, immersed in reading *Football Illustrated*, a publication previewing the upcoming college season. He was twelve and a first-class sports junkie.

During a break in the bridge game, Kletzing talked about parent complaints over a lack of high school sports coverage in the *Enterprise*. He said he didn't have anyone available to help him solve the problem. Then he turned in Bob's direction.

"Bobby, how would you like to try covering the football games for me this fall?" Kletzing asked. He got a positive response, and that's how Robinson's sports writing career began. His stories, by his own admission, were on the primitive side at first but gradually improved. A sixth-grade teacher accused him of having one of his parents write the stories for him. The insult stung, but he swallowed his pride and, wisely, didn't tell her what he thought of her and her teaching approach.

He kept at it through high school, too, when he played on some of the teams he was writing about. Through it all, Kletzing kept pushing him toward a journalism career. For instance, he arranged for Bob to meet and do an interview with the New York Yankees' Bill Bevens shortly after the latter's near no-hit pitching performance in the 1947 World Series.

At the same time, Bob's father took him to numerous college football and basketball games at Oregon State University, the University of Oregon and Multnomah Stadium (now called Jeld-Wen Field) in Portland. The two also attended some pro tour golf tournaments in the state, including the 1955 Western Open at Portland Golf Club.

In 1947 and 1949, Kletzing somehow obtained press credentials for Bob to each of Oregon State's best-of-three basketball playoff series with UCLA for the Pacific Coast Conference championship. His seat in Oregon State's antiquated Men's Gym (capacity barely more than two thousand) was in the middle of the press section both years. He described it as an "awesome experience" to sit among writers from most of the major newspapers on the West Coast even though some of those writers gave the teenager funny looks.

Oregon State won both of those playoffs—incidentally, the one in 1949 with rookie coach John Wooden directing the Bruins.

That was the background that sent Robinson on to the University of Oregon School of Journalism, the *Eugene Register-Guard*, the *Capital Journal* in Salem, the *Oregonian* in Portland for thirty-seven and a half years and, finally, to freelance writing in his retirement years. Most of those years were spent covering sports, but he also spent time at the *Capital Journal* as assistant news editor and city editor, in addition to sports editor.

At the *Oregonian*, he had the golf beat for more than thirty years and also covered many other major sporting events. He was the beat writer for the Portland Trail Blazers when they won the NBA championship in 1977 and wrote two books on that experience—*World Champions* (Graphic Arts, 1977) and *Bill Walton—Star of the Blazers* (Scholastic Book Services, 1978). He wrote chapters for two other books: *Chicken Soup for the Golfer's Soul—The Second Round* (Health Communications, 2002) and *Red Hot and Rollin'* (Nestucca Spit Press, 2007).

In addition, he has written magazine articles for the *Pacific Northwest Golfer*, *Golf World*, *Golfweek*, the *U.S. Golf Journal* and *On the Tour*.

Robinson was selected by his peers as Oregon's Sportswriter of the Year in 1977. He also was honored for contributions to golf with the Peter Jacobsen Award in 1997, the Dale Johnson Media Award in 2003 and the Northwest Golf Media Association's Distinguished Service Award in 2004.

He resides in Portland with Donna, his wife of fifty-eight years. He also admits to wondering if this all would have happened without the kick-start from Ralph Kletzing.

Visit us at
www.historypress.net